Independent Scho

Meet the World

RETHINKING CAREERS, RETHINKING ACADEMIA

Joseph Fruscione and Erin Bartram, *Series Editors*

Independent Scholars Meet the World

Expanding Academia beyond the Academy

Edited by

Christine Caccipuoti and

Elizabeth Keohane-Burbridge

University Press of Kansas

Published by the University Press of Kansas (Lawrence, Kansas 66045), which
was organized by the Kansas Board of Regents and is operated and funded by
Emporia State University, Fort Hays State University, Kansas State University,
Pittsburg State University, the University of Kansas, and Wichita State University

Library of Congress Cataloging-in-Publication Data

Names: Caccipuoti, Christine, editor. | Keohane-Burbridge, Elizabeth, editor.
Title: Independent scholars meet the world : expanding academia beyond the
academy / edited by Christine Caccipuoti and Elizabeth Keohane-Burbridge.
Description: Lawrence : University Press of Kansas, 2020. | Series: Rethinking
careers, rethinking academia | Includes bibliographical references and index.
Identifiers: LCCN 2020006823
ISBN 9780700629909 (cloth)
ISBN 9780700629916 (paperback)
ISBN 9780700629923 (epub)
Subjects: LCSH: Independent scholars. | Learning and scholarship.
Classification: LCC AZ231 .I53 2020 | DDC 001.2—dc23
LC record available at https://lccn.loc.gov/2020006823.

British Library Cataloguing-in-Publication Data is available.

Printed in the United States of America
10 9 8 7 6 5 4 3 2 1

The paper used in this publication meets the minimum requirements of the
American National Standard for Permanence of Paper for Printed Library
Materials Z39.48-1992.

Contents

Series Editors' Foreword

*I*ndependent *Scholars Meet the World* considers a category of scholars that has long existed but has become increasingly important to consider in an academic job market that seems to offer fewer opportunities for permanent full-time work with each passing year. Christine Caccipuoti and Elizabeth Keohane-Burbridge have assembled a collection of essays that not only offers advice about being an independent scholar but also urges scholars of all sorts to reconsider what truly divides—and unites—us in our work.

The essays in *Independent Scholars Meet the World* are rich, insightful, and above all accessible. The editors have taken great care to assemble a group of writers who can speak to the ways gender, race, sexuality, marital status, and disability inform the experiences of independent scholarship. Just as in any writing about personal experiences, the stories these scholars have to tell do not provide a complete account of what it means to be an independent scholar, nor could they. Instead, they provide a series of important provocations designed to make you ask questions of your own experience and assumptions, whether you're working as an independent scholar, considering it as a possible career path, or teaching and researching in a tenure-track academic position.

To Christine and Elizabeth, the lives and careers contained in the pages of this collection demonstrate the need for a revision in terminology and mindset: "What we in this work do is not an alternative to academia—it is an expansion of academia. We in the expanded-ac world use our skills, knowledge, and connections to bring academia to a broader audience. We need to widen the umbrella of academia and acknowledge that independent scholars have a vital role in it."

As series editors, we have sought out books and perspectives that do exactly that: expand our understanding of academia, its members, and its possibilities. No matter where you are on your academic journey, we hope *Independent Scholars Meet the World* helps you imagine—and create—a wider expanded-ac world.

Joseph Fruscione and Erin Bartram

"You Just Do It": A Foreword

BEN RAPHAEL SHER

I'm one of the people that Elizabeth and Christine mention in their introduction, who initially declined to contribute to the book. I was between jobs at that point, devoting all of my time and energy to getting the next thing, and didn't have the resources to take on a project for which I wouldn't get paid. I was thrilled that, when they asked me if I wanted to write the foreword, I had a job and could say yes. Such are the joys and sorrows of leaving tenure-track dreams for the gig economy. Whenever I hear somebody tell the narrative about how their career developed, I always get annoyed because it seems like a lot of random things just happened to them and they got lucky. I did not trust that to happen to me, which is one of the fundamental reasons that I chose a career in academia: it seemed to offer a reliable path. In the end, the path didn't go where I expected that it would, and a lot of random things just happened to me and I got lucky. At the same time, leaving the traditional academic road, and finding something else, made me wonder if randomness and luck are actually things that you consciously and subconsciously create.

I'm not going to talk too much about my eight years in graduate school because it was enough to experience them once. Like this book's contributor Allyson Schettino, I embarrassingly thought that it would be as utopian as my small liberal arts college, and that I'd get to spend the rest of my life thinking and teaching about things that were important to me: cinema and media, and how they get intertwined with society, politics, and people's day-to-day lives. One beloved undergrad mentor warned me that this would not be the case, the other told me that if I worked hard and had integrity I would get a tenure-track job. I possibly listened to the wrong mentor.

Nonetheless, graduate school offered a lot of joys: I had deep, intellectually and emotionally stimulating relationships with certain professors and classmates, I taught seminars on four of the subjects that I care about the most deeply (LGBTQ media spectatorship, movie musicals, American genre films' representations of trauma, and how to teach and mentor undergraduates). I fell in love with most of the hundreds of students that I taught as a TA and an instructor. I became president of UCLA's graduate student–run film society, The Crank, and hosted some great filmmakers, including Crispin Glover and Stephanie Rothman. I received a distinguished teaching award, which is still one of the life events that means the most to me. I once read every issue of, like, twenty-five magazines from 1970 to 1980 to piece together the history of an obscure Norman Lear comic soap opera about gender role reversal called *All That Glitters*, which was the most fun I ever had. I wrote a dissertation titled "Fraught Pleasures: Domestic Trauma and Cinephilia in American Culture," which explored how people use their profound, obsessive love of films, TV, and popular culture to process experiences of trauma, and published a couple of anthology chapters based on its concepts. It was a topic that meant a lot to me personally, and that I really wanted to understand. Many people didn't know what I was talking about when I started conceptualizing the project, and I had to fight to make them believe that it made sense. Now, I feel like I see Buzzfeed think pieces on this topic every week, which, unfortunately, have nothing to do with my work. Still, writing this, it sounds like I had a pretty successful graduate school career—I'd probably be annoyed if somebody else wrote it and think to myself, "Well, don't you think you're great?" While it happened, I felt like a failure a lot of the time (especially in comparison to many of my inhumanly productive and brilliant classmates), I had to hustle every quarter to get together enough jobs and fellowships to barely make ends meet, and I—like most graduate students—dealt with some profound challenges, which induced a lot of anxiety, depression, and maybe even a touch of PTSD. I'll tell you about that in person if you ask me. When it was over, I couldn't get a job. Let's really begin there.

When I went on the job market during the 2014–2015 school year, I believe that there were about twenty-five jobs for probably thousands of applicants in my field. Maybe ten of the job descriptions made it seem like I could feasibly get an interview—half of which were a stretch. I did not get one. I saw people who graduated in the years before me getting increasingly frustrated as they worked as adjunct professors or, as contributor Katherine Anderson Howell effectively puts it, "road scholars," each one having to drive all over Los Angeles teaching at multiple universities, grading hundreds of papers, and earning poverty-level wages. I got disturbing advice. One professor told me that you should only adjunct for a year or two, otherwise you'd get "a stink on you," and hiring committees for tenure-track jobs wouldn't interview you because they'd wonder why nobody else had hired you. Since the job market seemed to mandate that people adjunct for years and years, this frightened me. It was also wrong. Several of my friends who did stick it out as adjuncts and visiting professors got the great jobs that they deserved years later. Another professor told me that I would eventually get a tenure-track job, I would just have to "wait and be patient" while adjuncting for years. In addition to finding this advice confusing—it directly contradicted the "stink" argument—I found it annoying. For eight years I had worked multiple jobs to scrounge together a $15,000–$25,000 annual income, and still had to take out a lot of student loans and get help from my parents because the cost of living in Los Angeles is so high. Logistically, I didn't feel that I could do it for two, three, or five more years, knowing that the chances of getting a tenure-track job would remain minuscule. Also, I just knew that driving to five different colleges and grading a thousand papers a semester would drive me insane. Unlike my many genius, tireless friends who did it, I was sure that it wouldn't work because of my personality.

Another common bit of wisdom was that, circa 2015, nobody could get a tenure-track job straight out of graduate school, and that you had to get a post-doc or visiting professor position first, usually in a different city. Like Elizabeth Keohane-Burbridge, between 2007 (when I entered graduate school) and 2015, I fell in love with Jason, got engaged, and started a family (we adopted two cats, who are the center of our lives). If I was honest with myself, I knew that I wanted a happy long-term relationship more than anything. The day that Jason proposed to me, after I said yes, one of my first thoughts was, "Finding a great guy who wants to marry me, who I want to marry, was infinitely harder than writing a dissertation." I knew several academic couples who made long-distance relationships work. In this book, Joshua Hevert aptly demonstrates how a couple can successfully navigate a long-distance relationship, and the challenges, and opportunities, that arise when one moves for one's partner. However, neither of these options felt feasible to me. I could not make Jason move and rebuild his career in a new place if it would only be temporary, and I wanted to see him and my cats every day and spend every weekend with them. They made me much happier than academia. Many in academia feel that you should be willing to sacrifice a relationship and personal life for your career. One person told me that her dissertation chair advised her to send a letter to her friends and family telling them that she would not have time to communicate with them during the year that she was on the job market. I knew a woman whose dissertation chair—a famous scholar—severed ties with her because she got pregnant (not unlike contributor Danielle T. Slaughter). I felt very 1950s, but I knew in my bones that I would rather change careers completely than leave my family for long periods. I feel very grateful that my own dissertation chair, Kathleen McHugh—who was always supportive, no matter what path I took in my life and my work—validated my decision. Other dissertation chairs, take note: such support matters a great deal.

So I needed to make a living, and the short-term options for academic employment were untenable. I think that, underlying these practical problems, was the fact that I didn't love being an academic enough to make more sacrifices. For years, there had been a very quiet whisper from the bottom of my soul telling me that I wanted to do something else, and that it might involve the seeming impossibility of working in the entertainment industry. I had squelched it. Now I told myself, and maybe the universe, that I was going to have to be creative and make something else happen. Since movies and TV were (other than Jason and my cats) my great loves, I should probably start there.

Reading this volume, I find it tremendously comforting how many people talk about finding themselves in an abstract, black space when they decide to leave academia, at least in its standard form. Alison Innes writes: "The thought of leaving was like staring into a bottomless black pit." Dayanna Knight writes: "I often dreamt of falling, always falling, into the dark." I kept thinking to myself, "My career is like a bombed-out black pit." I called everybody I knew who worked in the entertainment industry, and none of them could help. I sent out a bunch of résumés, and heard nothing back. Like many authors in this book, I felt that my long academic career was basically incomprehensible to everybody outside of academia. If I wanted to work in the entertainment industry, I should have started as a PA or an assistant when I graduated from college, and built up the necessary experiences and connections. Like Alison Innes, I worried that people would stamp me with the dreaded "overqualified but underqualified" label. At one point, I gave up and decided that I would become a road scholar and seek adjunct work after all. I couldn't even find one of those gigs, since many of the cinema and media studies PhDs from Los Angeles universities who had graduated since the economic crash of 2008 without tenure-track jobs were filling them. I felt incredibly hopeless and despairing, and was afraid that I wouldn't be able to support myself. Even though Jason had a stable income, in LA we needed two in order to pay the rent and eat.

One of the things that kept me sane throughout graduate school was regularly getting together with a group of friends who had nothing to do with academia. In that group, we all came from disparate walks of life, but we understood each other because many of our shared experiences helped us process the world in similar ways. I could be honest about what I was going through with them, and get empathy in return. It was the opposite of academia, where you're often told that revealing personal struggles and vulnerability will harm you, and that you have to wear a sort of armor of confidence and success to be accepted. I often felt guilty doing less reading or less research in order to spend time with friends, but I always made time for it because it helped me so much. It felt like the thing that I did to *get away* from my career. At one of these get-togethers, I got my "big break."

One of my friends introduced Andrew to the group. He was a former FBI agent who had become a writer and executive producer on a popular television series about the FBI. Because of his unusual history, he knew that the skills you develop on one career path can help make you an unusual but maybe extraordinary choice for a job on another career path. One day while we were hanging out, after I had bitched and moaned about how I would never get a job and my life was a failure (*not* a good networking tactic!), he came over to me and said that he was starting a small production company and needed somebody to help out. He knew that I knew everything about TV and movies, and wanted to talk about the possibility of working together. This is what I'm talking about when I say that people's careers are often composed of random lucky events. Who can plan or strategize something like that? At the same time, this person wouldn't have been interested in talking to me if he didn't know that I had a PhD in cinema and media studies, and if he didn't like the complicated person he had come to know. I've come to think that sometimes just *insisting* on doing the things that make you feel whole is its own kind of planning, its own kind of strategy. I think about the intimidatingly impressive contributor to this book Vay Cao, who writes: "If you want to make your professional life easier while you are in graduate school, diversify, diversify, diversify your time." This is useful advice—but I want to add something. Sometimes diversifying your time means that you won't be able to do all of your seminar reading one weekend, or your research for a paper will be just a little less in-depth, and often it's worth doing it anyway. Taking time to feed all parts of yourself in graduate school, and on the job market, is the only way to thrive—even if you have to prioritize your needs over somebody else's.

I went for a job interview with Andrew. He told me that his

production company was dedicated to making movies and TV shows about law enforcement that were more accurate than most entertainment because they were created by actual law enforcement professionals. He knew everything about crime and law enforcement, and he wanted to work with someone who knew everything about media. I assumed he wanted to hire me as his assistant, which was fine with me. I was shocked when he told me that he wanted me to be the company's vice president of development. I honestly didn't even really know what a vice president of development did, but I had just read Sam Wasson's biography of Bob Fosse. Fosse was just a dancer when somebody asked him if he could choreograph a summer stock musical. He had no idea if he could, but he said yes. So, I figured that this was my Bob Fosse moment, and I said that, yes, I was totally prepared to take on that role.

So, for the next three years, this neurotic musical queen spent his career developing TV series with a bunch of former criminal profilers, forensics analysts, police chiefs, and spies. Graduate school had taught me how to balance ten different projects/jobs at once, how to take concepts and present them in a fun and accessible way to students and peers, how to work with a wide array of strong personalities, how to help students to communicate their ideas persuasively through their work, and how to critically analyze films and TV shows. These skills served me in good stead when trying to get twenty different shows green-lit, working with writers and filmmakers to develop their projects, writing and presenting pitch materials, and deciding which script submissions we should try to get made. Who knew?

The transition wasn't easy. For the first year, several of Andrew's entertainment industry colleagues overtly called me an impostor who didn't have the appropriate experience to be trusted. Of course, I believed them. Thankfully, Andrew did not. Eventually, we developed a documentary series with Emily (one of his colleagues who *did* like me), and sold it to CBS. The series was a smash hit (we beat *Dancing with the Stars* and the Emmys in the ratings!). Emily joined the company as SVP of development, and we developed another documentary series and sold it to another major network. This time, I asked to work on the show as an associate producer, to get the much-needed on-the-ground experience that I'd missed. After a few years, I had a couple of recognizable credits on my résumé, and people no longer questioned whether I belonged.

Emily became an invaluable mentor and close friend. She knew that I had a passion for horror films, and that a big part of my dissertation was about how people processed trauma through their love of horror. She emailed me an article stating that a company headed by one of her friends was producing a six-part documentary series for the AMC network called *AMC Visionaries: Eli Roth's History of Horror*. She just thought that I'd be excited to watch it, but a lightbulb went off in my head: I had to work on this show. To make extra money during graduate school, I had written listicles about horror movies for various websites (Chiller TV and Shout! Factory). I had a portfolio of articles with titles like "Horror Movies with Great Dance Sequences" and "The Greatest Canadian Horror Movies." I loved writing these articles because, like alt-ac writing and podcasting did for Christine Caccipuoti and Elizabeth Keohane-Burbridge, they allowed me to have a voice and write directly from my very specific sensibility. I was lucky that these qualities in my writing were encouraged by many of my professors, but they were often discouraged by journal peer reviewers. Again, during graduate school, I sometimes worried that writing these listicles, though fun, satisfying, and financially helpful, took too much time away from my academic career. Years later, when I wrote a letter to the executive producers of *Eli Roth's History of Horror* telling them that I was the best person to produce the series, I had twenty fun, quick, easy-to-read articles that I could send them as proof. I never expected to hear from them, but I did. When I went for a job interview, I was surprised to find that the showrunner, Kurt Sayenga, seemed a lot like a professor; he specialized in documentaries that were stylish, entertaining, and academic at the same time, and was deeply interested in the various connections between films and trauma. When I got the job and started working on *History of Horror*, it seemed like all the crazy, somewhat random strands of my career finally came together and made sense.

One of my jobs on the show was to write questions for our many interview subjects, who included personal heroes like Jamie Lee Curtis, Quentin Tarantino, Jordan Peele, Linda Blair, Tippi Hedren, Rob Zombie, Robert Englund, and Edgar Wright. I got to actually *conduct* an on-camera interview with my greatest hero of all, Heather Langenkamp, who played Nancy Thompson, Freddy Krueger's most formidable foe in *A Nightmare on Elm Street*. It was a nice full-circle moment because I had written about how Nancy had influenced my life in my application essay for my MA program. My boss, Kurt, also allowed me to choose and book many of our "horror experts," which I found tremendously exciting, as I had the opportunity to include the voices of both tenure-track professors whose work I loved (Jen Moorman, Jason Middleton), and independent scholars or scholars still on the job market whose work I believed to be on the cutting edge of the field (Kier-La Janisse, Chris Dumas, Amanda Reyes, Murray Leeder, David J. Skal, John Edgar Browning). Because Kurt was interested in my dissertation topic, we asked many of the interview subjects about the relationships between horror film spectatorship, filmmaking, and trauma. They had deeply insightful answers, and were inspired to talk about the genre in ways that they hadn't before. As a result, the ideas in my dissertation became core thematic concepts of the show. I was thrilled beyond belief when the series aired and the critic for the website BlackGirlNerds, Sezin Koehler, wrote: "While it does have humorous moments, the general tone of *History of Horror* is one of an almost religious reverence and extreme respect for how this genre has helped individuals . . . [allowing] people to talk about difficult life experiences, like grief, trauma, and death."[1] Susan Leighton, at 1428Elm.com, wrote: "The 2018 AMC series was like taking a course in the origin of all the familiar conventions with the masters. Roth and the network did a fine job of turning a documentary series into a work of art. The amount of research that went into this undertaking celebrating horror in all its many forms is staggering."[2] I found it heartening that a lot of critics and film fans on social media compared the series to a film course. Maybe I was getting to disseminate my academic work as a teacher and an author after all, just not in the way I had expected.

I have to admit that when Elizabeth and Christine first approached me I was surprised that they wanted me to contribute to a book about being an independent scholar. "I'm not a scholar anymore," I thought to myself. "I *left*!" Reading this book has been healing for me because I've realized that leaving traditional academia does not necessarily mean divesting yourself of your identity as a scholar. In retrospect, I had thought about it that way because I had internalized "independent scholar stigma," which several contributors effectively and painfully outline. These authors correct that stigma and erasure by persuasively insisting that we have not left academia and our identities as scholars, but expanded them. For example, Laura A. Macaluso and Valerie Schutte demonstrate how being an independent scholar can allow you to participate in traditional institutions of academia (publishing, conferences), while also bringing your scholarship and expertise to other venues (for Macaluso, public exhibitions), and tailoring your job to meet your needs in a way that a traditional academic job often does not allow (for Schutte, not teaching and having time to do the work of full-time motherhood). I realize that, in my own way, I've done much the same. I've sometimes mourned giving up my identity as a scholar, which almost feels more biological than institutional. Reading this book has inspired me to own and celebrate the title "independent scholar." In many ways, I have worked hard for it. I correctly choose to wear that foolishly stigmatized adjective, "independent," as a badge of honor and a distinction. I feel like the characters at the end of *The Wizard of Oz*, finding out that they had what they needed all along.

That said, sometimes I feel slightly bittersweet about my work on *History of Horror*'s relationship to my earlier academic goals. A lot of my arguments, ideas, and sensibilities permeate the series, which is thrilling. But, unlike if I had written a book, the ideas are not obviously *mine*, nor are they only mine. On the show, they belong to Eli Roth, Kurt, our interview subjects, me, and all of the show's other creators. Most people watching the show have no idea who I am, or that I was involved! Certainly, if I tried to apply for a tenure-track job now, I probably wouldn't get an interview partly because I haven't written a book, even if the ideas from my dissertation are presented in a nationally televised documentary that reached 6 million people. At the same time, I'm sure that I wouldn't have reached a tiny fraction of those people with an academic monograph, and I know from reviews (and Twitter!) that the ideas about trauma, horror, and healing that are present in the show are revelatory and matter deeply to people, especially young people. One of the main points of my dissertation is that you can only understand films or genres by learning the perspectives of many people who are profoundly engaged with them. The documentary, even more than my dissertation, allows for exactly such an education. Furthermore, while producing it, I discovered that I prefer working on a team of brilliant, wonderful people on a project to writing by myself, and that I find the language of documentary filmmaking more conducive to the ways in which I want to express myself than academic writing. Usually, I've found, when you choose to do one thing over another, you often give something up but get something good in return. Because of the success of the series, we were renewed for a second season, and I was promoted to senior producer. I'm currently working on it now.

In writing the narrative of our lives, it is tempting to tell one of progress, to leave out the messy parts. It's also tempting to give yourself a happy ending. I could tell you that *Eli Roth's History of Horror* is mine. I *am* so proud of it that I do sometimes feel like if I never accomplish anything else in my career it will have been enough. But truthfully, it's more complicated than that. It took a year for *History of Horror* to get renewed for its second season, and during that time I spent months unemployed and feared that I would never work again. This coming April, my time will once again be done on the series, and *right now* I'm afraid that I'll never work again—that this last stretch will have been a lucky fluke.

In retrospect, my career trajectory has a narrative that makes some kind of sense. I hope that you won't read the chapters in this book and feel frustrated because your current career trajectory doesn't. I assure you that mine didn't feel like it was making sense while it happened, and sometimes it still confounds me. I've basically only included the good parts of my time in the entertainment industry, and have left out the toxic coworkers, the shows that almost sold and then didn't, the periodical "two steps forward, one step back" feeling, the jobs that I took to make money that didn't mean much to me. The gig economy is terrifying and complicated for everyone, and sometimes I wonder if it is particularly haunting for people who spent years and years building one career (in the case of the authors in this book, traditional academic ones), only to have it not work out. On my dark days, I think that if it could happen once, it can easily happen again, and this time I'll be even older. In the end, though, I always come to the conclusion that leaving academia—and then, ultimately, expanding it—gave me something more powerful than my anxiety and self-doubt: the knowledge that you can work toward something for eight years, have it not go where you planned, find yourself in a career that feels like a bombed-out black wasteland, and build something else, something better, from nothing. Flexibility, adaptability, and openness can get you very far, and they're like riding a bike (I actually don't know how to ride a bike; but I'm told that once you know, you don't forget). To me, the scary thing about leaving traditional academia is that I lost a defined track. One of the best things about it is that, when you don't have a defined track, you never know what's around the corner—it could be nothing, it could be terrible, but it could also be more wonderful and fulfilling than you ever dreamed, and that's exciting. Of course, for anybody reading this who chooses to pursue the tenure track, I think that it can bring scary and wonderful unpredictability, too. I think that maybe a career path that's perfectly stable and defined for the rest of your life, for somebody devoted to the humanities, is kind of like the tooth fairy, except you believe in it until you're in your twenties.

I wish that I could give you advice on how to succeed for the rest of your career. There are a lot of great tips in the coming chapters. My hope for you, as a reader of this book, is that you will find comfort in the similarities you share with these writers, learn from us what you can, and never compare your path to any of ours in a negative way. You will go your own way, to paraphrase Fleetwood Mac. You will have your own frustrations and miracles. I hope that you'll try to stay true to what you authentically want and need out of life, and take your own word as the last. However, rather than giving you practical career advice, I'll give you a few tidbits of wisdom on how to work at staying sane through the day-to-day madness of building a career, becoming an independent scholar, deciding to pursue the tenure track, or just being in the world, which I've picked up along the way. Tip one: on my way to work, there's a mailbox with writing on it that reads "Your life is under construction. Expect delays." This is true. This is insanely true. If you can accept delays, you'll feel better. I'm working on it. Tip two: I recently interviewed Ashley Laurence, who plays the heroine Kirsty in the seminal horror film *Hellraiser*. She defeats Pinhead and the demonic cenobites at the end of the movie, which is sort of like successfully changing careers. She's another of my lifelong heroes. She said that, in the film's climactic battle sequence, it was important to her that the character always be terrified, even when she acted most brave. When she said this, it stopped me in my tracks. I've always subscribed to the cliché that courage is not the absence of fear but the willingness to work through it. However, when she said that I realized that it is okay to also be the most afraid *during the very same moments* that you are the bravest. Success can still come from being terrified, as long as you don't let it stop you. Tip three: Elizabeth Taylor is the goddess, the ultimate role model, and a fearless iconoclast. You should hang up a picture of her and look to it whenever you need strength from someone who, like you, consistently went against the grain and accepted and celebrated her own eccentric authenticity (Google how she became a tireless AIDS activist when practically nobody else would, if nothing else).[3] She once spoke about how to get through life, and in my opinion her words are the only ones that you need: "You just do it. You force yourself to get up. You force yourself to put one foot before the other, and God damn it, you refuse to let it get to you. You fight. You cry. You curse. Then you go about the business of living. That's how I've done it. There's no other way."[4] This also applies to finding the professional road that you're meant to take. There are no endings, happy or not, until maybe death. There is only the business of living. I hope that this book will let you know that if you are currently occupying your own abstract black space, your own bombed-out black hole, you are not alone. Let's hold hands and help each other build toward the light. We just do it. We can. We should. The world needs us.

NOTES

1. Sezhin Koehler, "BGN TV Review: 'Eli Roth's History of Horror,'" BlackGirlNerds website, article posted November 27, 2018, https://blackgirlnerds.com/bgn-tv-review-eli-roths-history-of-horror/.

2. Susan Leighton, "Schools in Session! *Eli Roth's History of Horror* Tapped for Season 2," 1428Elm website, article posted December 16, 2020, https://1428elm.com/2019/11/08/eli-roths-history-of-horror-season-2/.

3. Start with "Elizabeth Taylor on HIV/AIDS" (YouTube video), Elizabeth Taylor AIDS Foundation, posted February 6, 2015, https://www.youtube.com/watch?v=vrsHv9eCCko.

4. J. Randy Taraborrelli, *Elizabeth* (New York: Warner Books, Hachette Book Group USA, 2006), 458.

Independent Scholars

Meet the World

Introduction:
Finding and Defining the Independent Scholar

CHRISTINE CACCIPUOTI

and

ELIZABETH KEOHANE-BURBRIDGE

"Independent scholar" is such a vague, amorphous term, isn't it? It means many things to many people and there is often a relationship between the varying definitions and the speaker's proximity to academia. The most common usage seems to indicate one who is a specialist in a field or subject but works outside of traditional academia.[1] The types of nontraditional jobs occupied by independent scholars increase every year, as fields like museum education and high school teaching are joined by newer options, from podcasting to even creating historical coloring books. No longer is a specialist tied to the employment trajectory followed by those of the last generation, and treading this new ground can be exciting, scary, or a combination of the two, depending on how you first encounter the concept of the independent scholar. This book contains both those who actively sought the nontraditional and those who hoped for a traditional professorial job and later changed paths. They are bright, accomplished, and to be admired. These are success stories that we hope will broaden the horizons of all those who encounter this collection. Yet, like all successes, they were not achieved without encountering difficulty. You see, independent scholars are often assumed to be either people without advanced degrees or people with advanced degrees who failed in achieving tenured professorships. These presumptions often cause traditional academics to discount the years of work many independent scholars have put into becoming specialists in niche areas. This can manifest itself in bizarre ways, such as when independent scholars attend academic conferences or talks or meetings. The lack of a university-level affiliation on their name tag signals them out to self-appointed gatekeepers as less-than, or potentially even a *gasp* hobbyist.[2]

The contributors to this volume know this scenario well and have shown that being persistent in the face of unwelcome naysayers is the key to coming out the other side confident in your place in the world. We (Elizabeth and Christine, your coeditors) have certainly experienced such negativity, and part of our reason for working on this collection is to help people understand that independent scholars and traditional scholars share an important quality: they are all scholars.

In 2017, Elizabeth attended a small conference at Oxford University relevant to her dissertation research. She had defended her dissertation in August 2016 and graduated in May 2017. Elizabeth requested that her name badge include both her podcast (see our chapter in this collection: *"Footnoting History for the Public"*) and the name of the secondary school at which she teaches. The conference organizers dropped the podcast and just included the school. As she stood in a small circle of tenure-track professors, postdocs, and graduate students, Elizabeth was asked about the school and comments were made about how nice it was that she could indulge her hobby by attending. The fact that Elizabeth was one of the conference presenters and had published in a peer-reviewed journal made no difference to these academics. They made it clear that she hadn't made it, most likely due to some internal lack, and that her work, therefore, couldn't and shouldn't be taken seriously. Elizabeth considered: hadn't she treated independent scholars in a similar way at previous conferences? Made polite comments while looking for "real" academics with whom to network and never believing that the independent scholars were also worth connecting to?

This stigma attached to the title of "independent scholar" is not new. For a long time, the term was relegated to those who did not have an advanced degree but had become a specialist on their own (there was even *The Independent Scholar's Handbook: How to Turn Your Interest in Any Subject into Expertise*, published in 1982). While one of the earliest discussions of being defined as an independent scholar was published in 1994, it is only more recently that a number of academics have begun to reflect on how the term "independent scholar" impacted those with academic training but who had left the university setting.[3] In June 2016, when Julie R. Enszer wrote "What Shall I Call Myself?" for *Inside Higher Ed*, she expressed the view that "for now, however, Independent Scholar feels like a statement of defeat: independent, because I was unable to secure an academic position."[4] This view, while upsetting, is one that is widely shared by scholars who hold this title as they struggle for acceptance from their tenure-track and already-tenured colleagues, fight to get published, and overcome the difficulties of researching without an institutional affiliation. In 2017, Megan Kate Nelson continued the conversation with her article "Stop Calling Me 'Independent Scholar'" for the *Chronicle of Higher Education*. She argued that there are no independent lawyers, nor independent businesswomen; they are merely lawyers and businesswomen without a qualifier, so why should independent scholars not merely be scholars?[5] The term "independent scholar" has often been used in academic circles as a means of marginalizing those who—by choice or necessity—specialize in a topic that fits within an academic field and yet work outside of the tenure-track professoriate. The gatekeeping extends to conference badges and to the popular website for scholars, Academia.edu (https://www.academia.edu/), in which members are categorized not by their specialty or interest but by their affiliation. Elizabeth, therefore, is listed by the name of the school where she teaches, while Christine's affiliation is our podcast, *Footnoting History*. "Independent scholar" is a listed choice in lieu of an affiliation, but is seemingly rarely used—as of January 2018, Academia.edu stated that it had 57 million members and, yet, as of the writing of this chapter, only 729 are listed as independent scholars.[6] One of our major goals with this collection is to heavily contribute to shifting away from the negative connotations associated with the term by showcasing the successes of independent scholars.

Defining "Independent Scholar"

When we decided to coedit this volume, we set parameters for the independent scholars we would include. As our volume is intended as a volume in the Rethinking Careers, Rethinking Academia series, we adhered to the description set forth by Joseph Fruscione and Erin Bartram on the University Press of Kansas blog: "Topics should speak to graduate students, recent and experienced PhDs, university faculty and administrators, and the growing alt-ac and post-ac community."[7] While we fully believe that years of study outside of a degree program can provide a person with expertise in a specialized area, this work is part of a larger series for those with academic training. To us, the expectation that employment "could" be within a university-level classroom commences when one receives an MA/MS (typically the point of specialization, such as when we went from general history students to specialists in the medieval period); because we are seeking to cover people who did not take the expected path, we felt it would be an ideal defining line for this particular collection. Although we do not believe that this definition is the only one for "independent scholars," this series is highlighting this specific community of independent scholars and our contributors were sought with these parameters in mind.

We wanted contributors who have advanced degrees in their fields but have not entered the tenure track (for any reason) and who are currently working in a role that is not traditionally academic but is still related to the field for which they attended graduate school. We limited our search to those in North America, understanding that the experiences of those who have left academia vary greatly by region. When we spoke of who would contribute, we imagined our group would include different fields, races, religions, life experiences, sexual identities, and sexual orientations. So what happened? We set out starry-eyed, believing our group would be fully inclusive and representative of the state of the field. To be fair, we shouldn't have been surprised about the turns our search for contributors took, given the many articles and studies about "alt-ac" over the past decades, but there was admittedly a sense of shock that accompanied discovering the general makeup of the community firsthand. So what, then, does an attempt to have an inclusive collection look like?

Throughout this process, we released our call for papers (CFP) on Twitter, Facebook, and LinkedIn, among others, hoping to achieve a cohort representative of our aspirations. We asked people to share the CFP on social media and through other networks. We compiled an initial list not limited to but including men, women, those in the humanities, the sciences, people of color (POC), museum educators, and activists, and then we started emailing. At least two independent scholars we approached had sworn off working for free in exchange for "exposure." We wouldn't and didn't fault them for this decision. As scholars who still face financial precarity, they fairly chose to focus on efforts that would result in financial remuneration. Only one man responded positively to our proposal, but five women did. Seeing this gender imbalance, we worked to address it as we moved forward in the process. Joseph Fruscione, understanding our situation because he had encountered a similar gender disparity in his own work, forwarded us contact information for one man who had expressed interest in participating in the series and several women he believed might also like to join us, so we contacted each of them. Here, we again received acceptance only from the female scholars. The result was that only one male independent scholar reached out, so naturally we accepted him. At this point, we had two male and, not counting ourselves, seven female contributors. Additionally, all contributors were cis men or cis women. Academia can be a hostile environment for people who are transgender or nonbinary. As Zoie McNeill, who is nonbinary, explained, they had no choice to be an activist in their graduate program because they needed to protect themselves.[8] Alex Hanna, a transwoman and POC, described the difficulty transgender scholars face on the academic job market.[9] As of publication, academia and graduate programs are still not safe for the gender nonconforming. But while we understood (though deeply regretted) the lack of gender nonconforming voices in academia and independent scholarship, we were confused by the ratio of cis men to cis women. We sat back and considered what could be happening.

We realized that most of the independent scholars we knew in humanities were women and largely white, and therein lies one of the many problems of academia.[10] Given how much writing (so-called quit lit) has been done by women on the topic compared to men, we should have anticipated this. Whereas the number of women in graduate programs has increased and many programs have more female than male students, this trend does not continue to full-time professorships. Multiple studies have shown that even though over the past forty years the number of women attending graduate school has increased, there has been a much slower climb in the number of women who have tenure-track positions across the humanities or STEM.[11] We were left with two conclusions. First, within the parameters for our collection, more women are likely to be independent scholars. And, second, male independent scholars (as defined by the series) are fewer in number and may not be as comfortable taking on this stigma. Extrapolating from these, we deduced that women's increased likeliness of being independent scholars leads them to be the more common voices on the topic, perhaps partly because they have a larger community in which they find support when discussing the stigma. Meanwhile, more than one male independent scholar we solicited declined in part because they felt that academia would be retaliatory if they described their experiences. Whether or not this fear would be realized as a result of participation, it is understandable that this concern would loom large as academic gatekeeping is a running theme throughout this collection.

You may ask yourself, or us, we suppose: if we had two male contributors, why do we now have only one? Unfortunately, the contributor Joseph Fruscione suggested to us had to withdraw from the process about halfway through due to other responsibilities. We reached out to Joshua Hevert, who happily agreed to take his place. Then, our second male contributor also had to excuse himself from the work as he had academic (he was seeking a business degree) and family responsibilities that needed to be addressed. Unfortunately, our second contributor realized he could not complete his work for us toward the end of the process, and after speaking with our editor at the University Press of Kansas, we all agreed to move forward rather than delay the publication date our contributors had worked so hard to keep. It is important to remember that for the independent scholar, publications are not a part of our tenure file and must be done while balancing many other work–life responsibilities. So we fully understood when two of our contributors let us know they would not be moving forward, but we wish they had been able to do so as their stories are also important.

And now for the other elephant in the room: race. The majority of contributors—male or female—in our collection are white because the majority of academia remains white. Anecdotally, it seems that many POC, especially those who are Black or Latinx, choose (are steered toward?) career paths that result in a professional doctorate, such as education or psychology. It is assumed that these degrees will be applied in the field; they are not degrees in which one's goal is to remain in academia itself and achieve a professoriate.[12] Only two of our contributors are POC (although one of our male contributors who was unable to complete his chapters is also a POC). Between 1976 and 2008, the number of students of color enrolling in graduate work increased. In 2008, Black graduate students made up 12 percent of the graduate cohorts, Hispanic students 6 percent, and Asian/Pacific Islanders 7 percent. Overall, though, the majority of higher education degrees are still earned by white students (64 percent in 2008, for example).[13] Because these statistics also include professional distinctions, such as MBAs or education degrees, it is unclear how many of these students would have had the goal of remaining in academia as their path, but, when compared to the number of POC who are academics, the difference is striking. Black graduate students are the least likely to see representation of academics like themselves among full-time or assistant professors. Statistics on academic positions by race and ethnicity from 2016 clearly show how underrepresented nonwhite communities are at the faculty level:

For example, among full-time professors, fifty-five percent were White males, twenty-seven percent were White females, seven percent were Asian/Pacific Islander males, and three percent were Asian/Pacific Islander females. Black males, Black females, and Hispanic males each accounted for two percent of full-time professors. The following groups each made up one percent or less of the total number of full-time professors: Hispanic females, American Indian/Alaska Native individuals, and individuals of Two or more races. In comparison, among full-time assistant professors, thirty-five percent were White males, thirty-eight percent were White females, seven percent were Asian/Pacific Islander males, six percent were Asian/Pacific Islander females, and four percent were Black females. Black males, Hispanic males, and Hispanic females each accounted for three percent of full-time assistant professors, while American Indian/Alaska Native individuals and individuals of Two or more races each made up one percent or less of the total number of full-time assistant professors.[14]

In Danielle T. Slaughter's chapter ("Academia Didn't Have a Place for Me, So I Created My Own Academy"), she directly addresses the difficulty of being Black in a graduate program of white students *and* white faculty. Her experience is anything but atypical for Black graduate students, and the pressures of academia are compounded for students who are seen by many as the representatives of their race or ethnicity. Edray Goins writes openly about his experience being a Black mathematics professor, and although he didn't leave academia, he did leave his tenured position at a Research I school for a liberal arts college. In his piece, he explains multiple issues, including the "rampant social isolation" and "being tired of being the only one." It is exhausting being one of the only representatives of your race but it is also a common experience for Black professors as well as other POC who pursue tenure.[15] In

"Quitting While Black," Fatimah Williams, founder and CEO of Beyond the Tenure Track, explains that choosing to leave academia after receiving her doctorate left her feeling like she was letting down the Black community by not helping to break down barriers and serve as an example. Ultimately, though, she determined that earning her doctorate and achieving a professional position was already an empowering choice for her and for her community and that success for her did not have to include a tenured position.[16] Uché Blackstock, MD, explains in a piece for *STAT*, an online medical journal, that after spending nine years as a faculty member for medical programs and heading diversity initiatives, the racism and sexism—and fear of retaliation for calling out that racism and sexism—was finally enough and she left medical academia to start her own business, Advancing Health Equity.[17] Black academics, such as Eugene B. Johnson and Monica F. Cox, have taken to Twit-ter to offer community to Black graduate students and early career researchers in the hopes of providing them with a community and keeping them in academia.[18] Considering how white independent scholars were wary to publish in this work in case it hampered their career prospects or led to retaliation, we cannot help but think that Black independent scholars would have similar and legitimate reservations. POC who speak out on racism on their campuses do not feel safe—it is understandable that POC who are independent scholars would also be concerned about attaching their names to their experiences.[19] Our contributors, therefore, are representative of academia's harsh and unnecessary racial divide. In addition to broadening academia to include independent scholars, we look forward to the broadening of academy by race and gender.

Through our discussions with other independent scholars of all backgrounds (regardless of gender, sexual orientation, race, religion, etc.) we have learned that many of our experiences are universal. For example, this work highlights three women who became independent scholars for reasons related to parenting, but as more men become the default parent, this issue is less one of gender and more that of workplace culture. During our first discussion with Joseph Fruscione, Elizabeth and Joseph both explained that their evening availability to speak was limited by whether or not bedtime for their children was a success, immediately establishing a bond of shared experience despite a disparity in their gender. Much like this scenario, we feel the experiences shared within this collection will resonate with many people whose lives do not share every quality with the author.

We firmly believe that representation matters, and although we were initially quite disappointed with our failure to recruit writers along our idealized demographic lines, upon reading our contributors' pieces we were heartened by the universality of much of their experiences, including the aforementioned family obligations, mental and physical health concerns, expressions of a desire for something different, and grappling with the daunting notion of personal identity. It is one of our largest hopes that those who were not willing (or able) to tell their stories here will do so elsewhere once they have encountered those shared in the pages of *Independent Scholars Meet the World.* We do not seek to be the only place where independent scholars have a platform to speak, but we do seek to spark a broader conversation that brings other voices forward and assists in creating a supportive community that lifts independent scholars of all types up and offers support for those who hitherto felt they did not have a place to be heard.

History of Academia and Tenure in the United States

As historians, we believe it is important to provide context for our discussion. Academia and tenure are often seen as existing since time immemorial, and yet, the concept of tenure largely dates from

World War I and World War II. Initially, tenure (understood in academia to indicate a permanent post) was created by universities and adopted by certain public school systems to remove outside influences, especially opposing political views, in determining the hiring and firing of teachers. There were attempts in the late 1800s in the United States to limit the ability of influential university board members or donors to oust scholars with whom they disagreed; this problem or concern did not seem widespread because even around 1910, most professorships were considered permanent.[20]

The American Association of University Professors (AAUP)'s 1940 Statement on Principles of Academic Freedom and Tenure marks the point at which tenure would be recognizable to those of us in 2020.[21] Even then, though, it was only in the post–World War II period that tenure became a carrot with which to attract scholars to remain in academia as opposed to pursuing a potentially more lucrative career outside it. The massive influx of veterans taking advantage of the GI Bill to earn a degree in higher education was met by a lack of professors to teach them. Tenure—the promise of a permanent position—was used to keep those with graduate degrees teaching the returning soldiers. Many of these young men (for they were largely male, white, and Christian) would have remembered the time before the war and the Great Depression. A job from which they couldn't be fired as long as they put in seven years of effort (the probationary period) must have seemed like a golden opportunity even if the pay was less than they could find in other fields.[22]

Of course, this golden period was short-lived. The 1950s ushered in the second Red Scare, and loyalty oaths (one of which Elizabeth had to sign to adjunct at Georgia Perimeter in 2012) became the order of the day for those in many fields, including academia.[23] In fact, as Ernst Benjamin explained, by 1986, a third of academics supported abolishing tenure as it seemed not to encourage and protect new thought but to provide continual employment for those well past retirement age—sharply shrinking employment opportunities for younger scholars. Unsurprisingly, Benjamin, as the former general secretary of the AAUP, believes that it is folly to cast aside tenure, and, to be fair, that conversation is outside the scope of this work. But what attracts us here is his argument that the reliance of universities on non-PhD-holding adjunct labor is to blame for the number of PhDs unemployed in tenure-track positions.[24]

In 2007 in a *New York Times* article, Alan Finder raised yet another alarm about the decline of tenure and the adjunctification of academic labor.[25] We have seen since the 1970s that tenured university positions are on the decline. As of 2016, only 27 percent of higher education instructors were tenure-track or tenured, leaving a whopping 77 percent of university faculty, many of whom have PhDs, with insecure employment.[26] Adjuncts, especially, are low paid, receive no benefits, and have no job security—even a contract to teach does not guarantee that there will be a class (and pay) available. It is unsurprising, then, that many with MAs and PhDs are choosing to step aside from the professoriate and find alternative, dare we say independent, career paths. Of course, adjunctification impacts certain demographics with graduate degrees more than others.[27] While there has been an increase in employment opportunities for women and POC in higher education, these positions are often the part-time and underpaid adjunct positions described in our discussion of gender and race above and in the *Inside Higher Ed* article "More Faculty Diversity, but Not on Tenure Track."[28]

Academia Saves Itself?

For many inside and outside of academia, graduate school is portrayed as an extended adolescence, and the added loans matched with the low pay of a graduate stipend or fellowship can leave many academics a decade behind their peers financially. We have friends who ultimately left their programs at the proposal or "all but dissertation" (ABD) phase simply because they felt their lives could not continue on "pause" for any longer. So those who left must contend with knowing not only that many in their field view them as failures but also that those outside of academia perceive them as having spent the last four or more years trying to extend some sort of perpetual childhood. As we know, while grad school can feel like a substitute for childhood or adolescence, in reality it is an apprenticeship undertaken with the belief that, when it is finished, a tenure-track position will appear. What happens, then, when it doesn't? Further, what happens when a graduate-level scholar does not desire a tenure-track university job (as was Christine's experience)? What does success look like to those who do not participate in traditional academia when that is what they have been trained for? Well, this book is about that.

The goal of academia should be intellectual curiosity used to examine the past, present, and future in the hopes of better understanding the role of humankind and the physical and metaphysical world. Given this understanding, scholars with much to contribute cannot be shut out of the conversations because their conference name tags don't have the right schools on them. In the next ten chapters, we share eleven stories of academics who have chosen to pave their own ways outside of academia. They are using their skills and providing important contributions to their respective fields. Academia is at a crossroads: It can decide to barricade itself within the ivory tower and become everything of which it is accused *or* academia can save itself by bringing more scholars into the tent—scholars whom they themselves have trained. If, as we hope, it chooses the latter, it must not be done as a begrudging gesture of tokenism, but an admission that work outside academia not only has merits but is a necessary aspect of sustaining the field. In these pages, we set forth how different independent scholars have continued to walk the divide—may the insights shared here help future persons like ourselves and also the larger community understand the worth of work outside academia. We offer here a correction to the popular term "alt-ac." What we do is not an alternative to academia—it is an expansion of academia. We in the expanded-ac world use our skills, knowledge, and connections to bring academia to a broader audience. We need to widen the umbrella of academia and acknowledge that independent scholars have a vital role in it.

It is at this point in most prefaces that the works included are described individually or thematically, and although this preface is about straying from the traditional academic mold, this is one tradition we are happy to uphold. We simply asked our contributors to explain why they joined academia, why and how they became independent scholars, and what that has meant to them. We emphasized that their successes as independent scholars were what led us to want their voices in our collection, but that they should not hide their struggles. Multiple themes arose across contributors, although the gig economy, mental health, disability, family responsibilities, and reclaiming one's identity are arguably the most relevant or timely.

The gig economy is a relatively new term, like influencer or even, dare we say it, podcasts, but as with so many things "we know it when we see it."[29] For most of us, the gig economy calls to mind the business practices of Uber or Lyft, where people work as contractors for multiple companies to piece together a living wage. As David White of the *Los Angeles Times* suggested in early 2019 when discussing Uber, performers are possibly some of the first gig workers.[30] A film, television show, or play will all have an end, so although one might be contracted to it for the duration, there is no true permanent employment. Job security becomes even more precarious the lower you are on the performance ladder, and

Christine's years of working as a background actor (aka "extra") have made her intimately familiar with the gig economy: even when she is told she will work on a production for many days throughout the filming schedule, each day of work is not officially booked until the day prior. You are only guaranteed that one day, and it is more common than not to hear of background performers hustling to get another day of work on a different set in between takes on their current set of employment. Getting booked for multiple days at the same time can be akin to feeling like you won the lottery. While the job itself is necessary (imagine your favorite programs with completely empty streets, restaurants, or hospitals) and can be rewarding, there is great potential for burnout and few opportunities for guaranteed income for any known length of time. The gig economy is familiar to many academics in the form of adjuncting.[31] From graduate students to those with MAs or PhDs, many have pieced together work by teaching at numerous schools, and this aspect of the field is referenced in Katherine Anderson Howell's chapter. Elizabeth's high school students refer to it by an even older name: hustle. In our modern economy, to be able to hustle is pretty much expected, and that goes for our contributors not only during their time in academy but also since they left and began to build their own brands. In Allyson Schettino's and Alison Innes's respective chapters, each explains how museum work is often part-time until one reaches a certain and oft-coveted level, but until that point, a part-time position in a museum must be supplemented with other work to make a living wage. Dayanna Knight's contribution also reflects the complicated network independent scholars must weave in order to be able to pursue work that marries their academic passions with the reality of day-to-day concerns, like eating. Finally, Laura A. Macaluso's chapter details the impressive hustle that has allowed her to create her own consulting business with the goal of contextualizing and preserving monuments. While some who leave academia step directly into another position, often the career path—like many career paths— requires the independent scholar to be willing to do anything and be anything: a skill many independent scholars have mastered.[32]

Another common theme in many of our chapters is the negative impact of academia on mental health: from impostor syndrome to financial precarity to the constant need to be at the top of one's game while often receiving criticism that can cut to the bone. Graduate school and academia do not only create scholars—they can destroy them.[33] This struggle, often underfunded and ignored, is, therefore, not unique to independent scholars. In fact, nearly 40 percent of graduate students report experiencing anxiety and depression.[34] Leaving academia without having received the mental health support they needed, those in the expanded-ac world can find their mental health struggles compounded by feelings of failure. Choosing to leave or finding themselves outside of academia after a decade (between undergrad and graduate studies) of preparation to become tenure-track leaves scholars reevaluating their identity. Who are they? How do they see themselves? Was it all worth it? And earning your masters or doctorate doesn't suddenly make everything okay.[35] In her chapter, Allyson Schettino honestly and forthrightly explains the mental health crisis she experienced in graduate school and its impact on her choices then and now. Joshua Hevert reveals that, as he made the switch to high school educator while adjuncting and seeking teaching certification, he, too, needed to seek help for his mental well-being. While it does not come out in chapter 5, Elizabeth, as well, when she realized after her first year of teaching high school that not everyone perseverates on potentially negative comments for months, waking up in the middle of the night and experiencing insomnia, she also sought help—a step she now wished she had taken in graduate school when she just assumed that feeling like an incompetent failure was the name of the game.

Mental health overlaps with another topic that came up in some of our chapters: disability and accommodations. Alison Innes explains how academia is not set up for a person with a chronic illness.[36] Katherine Anderson Howell, who worked as a disability and accommodations coordinator at a university, realized quickly that her "flexible" position was anything but when it came to caring for her two children.

Finally, the wide spectrum of family responsibility is evident throughout. Katherine Anderson Howell, as mentioned, ultimately left the university setting because it did not allow her to care for her children. Valerie Schutte also made a similar decision based on the health of her child. Danielle T. Slaughter and Elizabeth, graduate students when they had their children, had to make choices when there was no leave and no money for child care. While women often become the default parent, more and more men are fulfilling this role and finding out how it can limit one's options in academia.[37] Joshua Hevert's chapter offers a different angle on family responsibility as his choices were strongly influenced by the "two-body problem" of academia: Who follows who when a tenure-track position is secured?[38]

In each of our chapters, our scholars deal with coming to terms with the label "independent scholar." There were unexpected negatives for those who wished to pursue research while adapting to their lives out of academia: they were cut off from access to university journals and books. In their chapters, Valerie Schutte, Christine, Elizabeth, and Joshua Hevert detail how they had to buy individual passes or ask friends to send them PDFs of works they needed to read because, without a home institution, the costs were often too high or, as Valerie Schutte explains, sometimes there was no choice as many databases assume only institutions want membership. However, adapting to this new label—that of independent scholar—has largely been positive, especially as many, such as Allyson Schettino, Alison Innes, Christine, and Elizabeth, realized that the skill sets they had developed for research and synthesizing arguments or for scaffolding information served them incredibly well on their chosen paths. And, of course, separation from the university setting and the demands to "publish or perish" left many of our contributors with more time to focus on public engagement. Allyson Schettino, Laura A. Macaluso, Alison Innes, Dayanna Knight, Danielle T. Slaughter, Christine, and Elizabeth all found themselves drawn to careers where the end result of research was not a footnote in someone's book, but direct engagement and practical interaction with interested learners.

Alt-Ac? Nah, We're Expanded-Academia

In this work, then, we offer you eleven stories of academics who have chosen a path that is more and more traveled and, yet, is still seen by many as a consolation prize for not quite making it. Each of our contributors, however, has made it. They are happily using the skills they learned in their graduate studies in their new careers. They are doing it on their own terms. Scholarship and ideas should not be generated by or for the select few who are employed in the professoriate. Keeping academic ideas only within the academy allows outsiders to forget the importance of these fields and to miss opportunities to become important contributors themselves. Increased approachability of academic experts can lead to increased dissemination of solid information in preference to, say, Wikipedia articles and internet conjecture. Above all, the recognition that independent scholars are truly scholars like their researching/ tenured colleagues would have a number of benefits: increased flow of information, sharing of resources, building of community, and revitalization of heavily incestuous fields. We hope this book contributes to a trajectory such that some day in the future people who pick it up will be surprised to learn that independent scholars were ever viewed as separate from those working in colleges or universities and that their value was ever questioned.

NOTES

1. Alternatives to this definition of "independent scholar" can be found, including Patricia Sullivan's chapter on independent scholars in which she addresses the myth that doctoral candidates work independently when writing their dissertations. She argues instead that graduate school should be seen as a creative community in which they work. Patricia Sullivan, "Revising the Myth of the Independent Scholar" in *Writing With: New Directions in Collaborative Teaching, Learning, and Research*, ed. Sally Barr Reagan, Thomas Fox, and David Bleich (Albany: State University of New York Press, 1994), 11–30. Similarly, Vicki Baker and Megan Pifer reference how one moves from the dependent status of doctoral student to that of an "independent scholar" after graduation. Vicki L. Baker and Meghan J. Pifer, "The Role of Relationships in the Transition from Doctoral Student to Independent Scholar," *Studies in Continuing Education* 33, no. 1 (2011): 5–17.

2. Practical issues facing independent scholars have been written about numerous times: Juliet Flesch, "Which Library is Mine? The University Library and the Independent Scholar," *Australian Academic & Research Libraries* 28, no. 3 (1997): 181–187; Christine Caccipuoti, "History's Information Access Barricades," *Christine Caccipuoti* (blog), entry posted August 23, 2018, http://www.christinecaccipuoti.com/post/2018/08/23/historys-information-access-barricade.

3. Laura Stempel Mumford, "Telling My Story: The Narrative Problems of Being an Independent Scholar," *Narrative* 2, no. 1 (1994): 53–64.

4. Julie R. Enszer, "What Shall I Call Myself?" *Inside Higher Ed,* June 21, 2016, https://www.insidehighered.com/blogs/university-venus/what-shall-i-call-myself.

5. Megan Kate Nelson, "Stop Calling Me 'Independent Scholar,'" *Chronicle of Higher Education,* October 8, 2017, https://www.chronicle.com/article/Stop-Calling-Me-Independent/241376.

6. Jefferson Pooley, "The Case against Academia.edu," *Chronicle of Higher Education,* January 7, 2018, https://www.chronicle.com/article/The

-Case-Against-Academiaedu/242141; "Independent Scholar," Academia
.edu, https://independentscholar.academia.edu/.

7. Derek Helms, "UPK Announces New Series: Rethinking Careers,
Rethinking Academia," *University Press of Kansas Blog*, entry posted
August 17, 2018, http://universitypressblog.dept.ku.edu/uncategorized
/upk-announces-new-series-rethinking-careers-rethinking-academia/.

8. Zoie McNeill, "Weird Academica: Life in Academia as a Non-
Binary Appalachian," *Activist History Review*, August 13, 2018, https://
activisthistory.com/2018/08/13/weird-academica-life-in-academia-as-a
-non-binary-appalachian/.

9. Alex Hanna, "Being Transgender on the Job Market," *Inside Higher
Ed*, June 16, 2016, https://www.insidehighered.com/advice/2016/07/15
/challenge-being-transgender-academic-job-market-essay.

10. Gianna Pomata, "Amateurs by Choice: Women and the Pursuit of
Independent Scholarship in 20th Century Historical Writing," *Centaurus*
55, no. 2 (2013): 196–219. Elizabeth also dedicated her dissertation to an
independent scholar who left academia to support her husband's career
and focus on her family; Elizabeth Keohane-Burbridge, "Dorothy Bruce
Weske: Academia and Motherhood in the Mid-Twentieth Century," *Nursing Clio*, December 1, 2016, https://nursingclio.org/2016/12/01/dorothy
-bruce-weske-academia-and-motherhood-in-the-mid-twentieth
-century/.

11. For example, see Sarah Winslow and Shannon N. Davis, "Gender
Inequality across the Academic Life Course" *Sociology Compass* 10, no. 5
(2016): 404–416; Donna K. Ginther and Shulamit Kahn, "Does Science
Promote Women? Evidence from Academia 1973–2001," in *Science
and Engineering Careers in the United States: An Analysis of Markets and
Employment* (Chicago: University of Chicago Press, 2009), 163–194;
Kristen Renwick Monroe and William F. Chiu, "Gender Equality in the
Academy: The Pipeline Problem," *PS: Political Science & Politics* 43, no.
2 (2010): 303–308; Nicholas H. Wolfinger, Mary Ann Mason, and Marc
Goulden, "Problems in the Pipeline: Gender, Marriage, and Fertility in
the Ivory Tower," *Journal of Higher Education* 79, no. 4 (2008): 388–405.

12. "Fast Facts: Race/Ethnicity of College Faculty," in National
Center for Education Statistics, accessed June 6, 2019, https://nces.ed
.gov/fastfacts/display.asp?id=61; Amelia Gibson, "This Is Your Pipeline
Problem," *Inside Higher Ed*, February 15, 2019, https://www.insidehighered

.com/advice/2019/02/15/far-reaching-effects-how-campuses-treat-senior
-faculty-color-opinion.

13. "Status and Trends in the Education of Racial and Ethnic Minorities," in National Center for Education Statistics, accessed June 7, 2019, https://nces.ed.gov/pubs2010/2010015/indicator6_24.asp.

14. "Fast Facts: Race/Ethnicity of College Faculty," in National Center for Education Statistics.

15. Edray Goins, "Why I'm Leaving a Research I University for a Liberal Arts College," *AMS Blogs: American Mathematical Society*, entry posted September 15, 2017, https://blogs.ams.org/inclusionexclusion/2017/09/15/why-im-leaving-a-research-i-university-for-a-liberal-arts-college/.

16. Fatimah Williams Castro, "Quitting While Black," *ChronicleVitae*, August 6, 2015, https://chroniclevitae.com/news/1088-quitting-while-black.

17. Uché Blackstock, "Why Black Doctors Like Me Are Leaving Faculty Positions in Academic Medical Centers," *STAT*, last modified January 16, 2020, https://www.statnews.com/2020/01/16/black-doctors-leaving-faculty-positions-academic-medical-centers/.

18. Eugene B. Johnson, "I want to start a thread: Black men who have PhD's or who are working on PhD's drop your discipline, your university, and your research interests. My hope is to build community specifically for black men who are attaining or have attained their PhD. #trynagrad #FirstGenDocs," Twitter, June 4, 2019, 12:55 p.m., https://twitter.com/eugenejohnson_/status/1135953172655214592?s=19. Monica F. Cox, "I'm starting a national network for Women of Color #WOC department chairs because I don't see resources targeting the issues we face daily. If you are interested in joining or contributing resources, please DM for more information or email cox.1192@osu.edu. #DeptChairLife," Twitter, August 20, 2018, 12:23 p.m., https://twitter.com/DrMonicaCox/status/1032302253007351808.

19. Andre Perry, "After Trump Victory, Black Professors Speak Out about the Routine Racism of Academia," *Hechinger Report*, November 11, 2016, https://hechingerreport.org/black-professors-speak-routine-racism-academia-trump-victory/.

20. Sol Gittelman, "Tenure Is Disappearing. But It's What Made American Universities the Best in the World," *Washington Post*, October 29, 2015, https://www.washingtonpost.com/news/grade-point/wp/2015/10/29

/tenure-is-disappearing-but-its-what-made-american-universities-the
-best-in-the-world/?noredirect=on&utm_term=.577c4a7ff8d2.

21. "Academic Freedom and Tenure," *Bulletin of the American Association of University Professors* 26, no. 1 (February 1, 1940): 49–54.

22. Gittelman, "Tenure Is Disappearing."

23. Rachel Levinson, "Academic Freedom and the First Amendment (2007)," in Presentation to the AAUP Summer Institute (2007), accessed June 7, 2019, https://www.aaup.org/our-work/protecting-academic-free
dom/academic-freedom-and-first-amendment-2007.

24. Ernst Benjamin, "Some Implications of Tenure for the Profession and Society," American Association of University Professors, accessed May 1, 2019, https://www.aaup.org/issues/tenure/some-implications
-tenure-profession-and-society.

25. Alan Finder, "Decline of the Tenure Track Raises Concerns," *New York Times*, November 20, 2007, https://www.nytimes.com/2007/11/20
/education/20adjunct.html.

26. "Data Snapshot: Contingent Faculty in US Higher Ed," news release, October 11, 2018, https://www.aaup.org/sites/default/files/10112018%20
Data%20Snapshot%20Tenure.pdf.

27. Rachel Kachchaf, Lily Ko, Apriel Hodari, and Maria Ong, "Career–Life Balance for Women of Color: Experiences in Science and Engineering Academia," *Journal of Diversity in Higher Education* 8, no. 3 (2015): 175.

28. Ronald G. Ehrenberg, "American Higher Education in Transition," *Journal of Economic Perspectives* 26, no. 1 (2012): 193–216.

29. Gianpiero Petriglieri, Susan J. Ashford, and Amy Wrzesniewski, "Thriving in the Gig Economy," *Harvard Business Review*, March/April 2018, https://hbr.org/2018/03/thriving-in-the-gig-economy.

30. David White, "Uber Should Take a Lesson from the Film Industry on How to Treat its Workers," *Los Angeles Times*, February 22, 2019, https://
www.latimes.com/opinion/op-ed/la-oe-white-gig-economy-workers
-film-uber-20190222-story.html.

31. Kim Tolley, ed., *Professors in the Gig Economy: Unionizing Adjunct Faculty in America* (Baltimore, MD: Johns Hopkins University Press, 2018); Herb Childress, *The Adjunct Underclass: How America's Colleges Betrayed Their Faculty, Their Students, and Their Mission* (Chicago: University of Chicago Press, 2019).

32. In 2020, the year of this book's publication, the tenuous nature of employment for gig and contract workers is being made particularly clear as a global pandemic caused by the spread of COVID-19 causes massive societal changes, including transitions to working from home, rampant business closures, and cancellations of scholarly events. Due to this, all scholars are currently facing increased limitations on where and how they can participate in their fields. While we cannot predict the long-term impact of the current health crisis, we have faith that independent scholars—like our contributors, as you will see in the following chapters— all possess skills of resilience and adaptability and will find ways to thrive in any future work formats.

33. Kate Bahn, "Faking It: Women, Academia, and Impostor Syndrome," *ChronicleVitae*, March 27, 2014, https://chroniclevitae.com /news/412-faking-it-women-academia-and-impostor-syndrome; Shayal Vashisth, "Graduate Students Face Challenges for Mental Health at Elite Universities," *Chronicle of Higher Education*, March 18, 2019, https://www.dukechronicle.com/article/2019/03/graduate-students-face -challenges-for-mental-health-at-elite-universities; Sally-Anne Gross, George Musgrave, and Laima Janciute, *Well-Being and Mental Health in the Gig Economy: Policy Perspectives on Precarity* (London: University of Westminster Press, 2018).

34. "More Than One-Third of Graduate Students Report Being Depressed," *Nature* 555, no. 691 (2018), https://doi.org/10.1038/d41586-018 -03803-3.

35. Anonymous, "The Invisible Injuries of Faculty Mental Health," *Inside Higher Ed*, August 31, 2018, https://www.insidehighered.com /advice/2018/08/31/removing-stigma-faculty-members-mental-health -disorders-opinion.

36. Nicole Brown and Jennifer Leigh, "Ableism in Academia: Where Are the Disabled and Ill Academics?" *Disability and Society* 33, no. 6 (2018), https://doi.org/10.1080/09687599.2018.145562.

37. Mary Ann Mason, "The Baby Penalty," *Chronicle of Higher Education*, August 5, 2013, https://www.chronicle.com/article/The-Baby -Penalty/140813; Ida Roland Birkvad, "Researchers with Children: a Disadvantage in Academia," *Science News*, January 11, 2016, https://www .sciencedaily.com/releases/2016/01/160111092607.htm.

38. Kelly J. Baker, "On 'Poor Husbands' and Two-Body Problems,"

ChronicleVitae, July 15, 2014, https://chroniclevitae.com/news/609-on -poor-husbands-and-two-body-problems; Matt Reed, "The Two-Body Problem Revisited," *Inside Higher Ed*, January 31, 2018, https://www .insidehighered.com/blogs/confessions-community-college-dean/two -body-problem-revisited.

PART ONE

INDEPENDENT ON CAMPUS

From Ancient Texts to Digital Tech

ALISON INNES

Academia is an exciting place to be, and graduate school is in many ways an all-consuming experience. We devote so much of our energy, time, and passion to our studies, and deciding to leave after completing an MA is difficult. We come to identify ourselves with our work as graduate students and with our field of study, and it can be hard to imagine what our identity might be outside of academia. I hope that reading my story will give you encouragement for your own journey, whether you are struggling with the decision to leave or have already made the leap. Leaving traditional academia doesn't mean you don't care about your field or discipline. You can still find ways to contribute and to explore your passion as an independent scholar.

Undergraduate Degree the First

You don't find classics, it finds you.

That's how my friend explained it to me once, and I have to

agree. I didn't set out to study the world of the ancient Greeks and Romans. In fact, aside from a grade ten Latin class in high school, I knew pretty much nothing about the Classical world until my third year of university.

Or maybe it was my fourth year. It depends how you count. My first year of university was at a small religious university-college. It was a nice, safe way to leave home and launch out into the world. I thought I wanted to study art, but then I also liked behind-the-scenes theater, and French was pretty fun, too. I think I changed my mind three or four times that first year, until I finally switched schools.

I didn't know much about linguistics when I decided to switch to a double major of history and linguistics at a different school. I was at home during February reading week that first year and came across a leaflet from Glendon College. A representative had visited our Ontario Academic Credit (OAC) (grade thirteen) French class, and when I looked at the leaflet again and saw that I could take linguistics, I knew in a flash that was what I wanted to do: not just study one particular language but learn about languages and how they work more generally.

Glendon College is a bilingual campus of York University in Toronto, Ontario, Canada. Glendon was located close enough to downtown that I could be "in the big city" when I wanted, but the campus itself was a beautifully treed former estate. About half of my credits didn't transfer, so I planned from the outset to take four full years. I loved that instead of just studying French, I could study in French. There was something incredibly novel about studying American history or women in the Renaissance in French.

I really loved my linguistics classes. Two professors in particular had such enthusiasm for their subjects that they kept my interest, even when the coursework wasn't my forte. I'm not sure if I ever had a good ear for phonetics (or maybe I did and lost it), but I took every one of Professor Greaves's classes. I also loved Professor Gutwinski, who, in between telling us stories of growing up as a child in Poland during the Second World War, taught us Systemic Functional Linguistics. And since Glendon was part of York, I took courses in historical linguistics or, eventually, ancient history, at the main campus as well. I'm not sure when I started to think about graduate school, but I know by my final year I was toying with the idea of doing an MA in linguistics.

But my MA wasn't to be until a decade and a half later and in a completely different subject, thanks to an experience I had while studying abroad. I decided during my second year at Glendon that I really wanted to spend a year studying in Glasgow. But when no one from Glasgow wanted to come to Canada, the exchange office gave me my second choice: Wales. I knew little about Wales, except it was a corner of the British Isles. Scotland and Ireland were the popular places for university students at the time; I liked the idea of going somewhere a little different, so I found myself in rainy but beautiful Swansea, Wales, living in a rather damp and aged student residence across the road from the beach.

I was focusing on linguistics and took courses in Welsh and in Egyptian hieroglyphs. Yes, seriously! They were exciting courses, although a lot of work, and subjects I couldn't study back home. I took my exchange year as an opportunity to explore subjects that weren't on offer at my home institution; since my grades for these courses wouldn't affect my degree back home, I could safely explore challenging subjects without worry.

The course that wound up changing my life, though, was Greek and Roman Science and Technology with Dr. Tracey Rihll. I took it because it looked like an interesting history course—I was growing unhappy with the stereotypical military and political history courses I had been taking for the history half of my double major. This course blew my mind wide open. Professor Rihll's love of her subject came across in every class. We weren't assigned readings from a textbook but were given a list of primary sources we could read from as we wanted. I remember devouring Herodotus and Pliny the Elder (whom I will always love) and stopping by Dr. Rihll's office to share the fascinating tidbits I found. My first paper for the course was on the manufacture and use of pipes for plumbing in the Greco-Roman world. I had only the vaguest understanding of Greek and Roman history (my only university-level classics course had been first-year Latin for fun), but I fell completely in love with their science and technology. Before I left Swansea that spring, I distinctly remember Dr. Rihll telling me that she would happily write a letter of reference for me to do an MA. I think I politely thanked her, but my mind was still thinking of my linguistics degree.

Having discovered the wonderful field of ancient history, however, I wasn't going to let it go entirely. I didn't want to switch programs to do a classics degree, since I was so close to completing my degree in history and linguistics. Instead, I registered for a few ancient history courses in my final year and got my grounding in the history of the ancient Greeks up to and including Alexander the Great. My fourth year flew by, and before I knew it, I earned my degree and was unleashed on the world.

Interlude: Or, I Try the Career Thing and Change My Mind

I was fortunate to land a job immediately, covering a maternity leave at a small museum near my hometown. I don't think I had necessarily dreamed about working at a museum—it was more of being in the right place at the right time. I had grown up with an appreciation for local history from my dad, who collected a variety of antique farm equipment and paraphernalia, and I had the key history skills—research and communication—and a little bit of experience from volunteering at Swansea University's Egyptian museum, so it seemed like a good fit. The position as education officer was part-time at a museum local to my family, which helpfully meant I could live with my parents while I was working. The museum had a small staff, and a new curator and registrar were both starting around the same time I was. It was a really good collective learning experience. The curator was very kind and took me under her wing, helping me learn the ins and outs of the job, and even sending me on an Ontario Museum Association three-day training course. My timing was good: I entered the museum field just as college museum programs were starting to gain traction in Canada. I was able to get into the field on the basis of my history degree and build experience on the job. My understanding now is that museum college programs are more common, making getting into museum work much more competitive. On the basis of the experience I built up there, I was able to hold two further museum jobs.

The work was tiring, but I loved it. I took on revising and developing education programs for schools, as well as organizing day camps for March break, summer holidays, and professional development days, when schools were closed for teachers' professional development opportunities. I worked on developing education policy, which I found enjoyable, and supervised high school volunteers.

When the first position came to an end, there was no doubt in my mind about continuing in museums. I interviewed at several museums around Ontario and eventually took a position at a historic house museum an hour away from family. It was exciting—my first full-time job, building a real career, buying my first car, living on my own.

The new job had a slightly different title but was much the same work. I had more experience, more confidence, and more freedom, but the staff there was even smaller. I found the job lonely and isolating at times; it was entirely possible in the winter, when tourism was quiet, to head into work and see no one all day and then go home. While I really enjoyed designing education programs and working with the summer university students, school groups and day camps were increasingly exhausting to lead, in part due to my chronic health issues.

I remember the day I decided to leave the job and go back to university. I was sitting in my tiny museum office, having just finished writing a new education program for fifth grade students about the science of sound. I looked around and wondered "Is this it?" Was this what I wanted to do for the next ten, twenty, thirty years—write and revise education programs? Lead countless tourists through the same tour? Wrangle countless children through the same education programs? It was important work, but was it really going to satisfy my own curiosity and desire to learn?

I was taking college night classes in American Sign Language at the time, and a friend there encouraged me to take the leap and pursue my MA dreams. I had talked about wanting to do an MA in classics, but I just didn't have the financial resources. So what? she said. No one has money in grad school. They give you money to do grad school. And why not do it sooner, rather than later?

The concept that I could get funding from the university to do a graduate degree was revelatory, and the kick in the pants Annabelle gave me was all I needed to begin looking at programs in seriousness. I didn't want to not try and then look back in regret and think of what might have been.

It quickly became apparent that my one year of undergraduate Latin was not going to be enough to get into an MA classics program. I would need to get a second BA. Fortunately, it would only require two years of full-time study, at least on paper. I chose the university where I thought I might want to do my MA and applied for a BA program.

Undergraduate Degree the Second: Things Get Serious

I'm glad I chose the university I did for my second undergraduate degree in classics. While my experience there was not a good one overall, I learned a lot about what I did—and didn't—want from a graduate program. Through my own undergraduate experience and my friendship with several graduate students, I learned the hidden curriculum—the unspoken rules of academia, the expectations placed on graduate students, and the hard work and commitment involved in getting a graduate degree at a Canadian institution. I also learned that the environment I was in was toxic for me. Grad school was going to be tough; I wanted to be in a place that was supportive and nurturing.

This degree program was my first experience of disability accommodation in academia. During my first degree, I was diagnosed with an invisible chronic pain condition that often brings a host of other disorders with it. I hadn't used any university support services during my first degree—if they existed at the time. Any accommodations or extensions I needed, I was able to work out with sympathetic professors.

By the time I started my second degree, I was more comfortable with my disability and with advocating for myself. I registered with the services for students with disabilities, worked with them to figure out what accommodations I needed, and communicated these with my professors. While academic accommodations can help level the playing field, they don't erase the disability. Unfortunately, dealing with chronic pain (and medications used to help manage it) affects one's concentration, ability to focus, and memory. I enjoyed courses where I could dig into a topic and explore it through research projects; however, courses that relied on memorization, such as Greek and Latin, were much more difficult.

I accepted that I would not excel in languages; my goal was to master them sufficiently so that I could research the things I was passionate about. In hindsight, it was my third-year Greek class that torpedoed any confidence I had with languages, and almost derailed my academic dreams. The focus of the class wasn't on understanding the selected Greek piece as a work of literature but on memorizing the correct translation from class and regurgitating it for an exam. Some people do very well with this—they have the type of brain that can quickly absorb and easily retain such information. My brain is not of this type, and despite hours of preparation, I was never confident with my translations.

Just how badly I was struggling did not become apparent until six days before the final exam. The final mark was based on a midterm and a final. The midterm was returned three days before the end of the semester, and while I wasn't expecting to have aced it, I was devastated to find I had failed it. There was no earthly way I could pull my grade up to passing the course in six days, let alone do well enough to not destroy my grad school dreams.

I sat in the academic advisor's office fighting back tears. Had I received any grades by the drop-by date in October? No. Had the instructor talked to me about how I was doing in the course at any point? No. I had received no feedback whatsoever until this point. Ironically that turned out to be my saving grace. Because I hadn't been given a certain percentage of my mark by the university's course drop date, the academic advisor was able to give me a retroactive withdrawal, which at least spared me the trauma of a final exam.

Despite this, I persevered. I knew languages weren't my strength, but I saw them as tools I needed to master so I could study the things I was really passionate about—like ancient medicine, social history, archaeology. I forged some strong friendships that helped sustain me through my MA and, later, through my transition away from the traditional academic route. My favorite courses were in ancient art and archaeology, and material culture—the things people left behind in the archaeological record—connected with my interest in ancient science and technology. The mundane facets of everyday life, like pipes and plumbing, made people from the ancient world real, and I wanted to learn more about what they thought and felt and the ways in which they lived.

Growing and Thriving

Maybe it was Dr. Rihll's confidence in me and my skills, maybe it was sheer stubbornness. Whatever it was, I applied for grad school and got in. Instead of remaining where I got my second BA, I sought a place that would help me grow as an academic.

I found that place at Brock University, Canada. I was amazed at the quality of the pedagogy and the supportive approach professors took, especially in teaching languages. Several professors took those of us with weaker language skills under their wing for extra attention. With time, the positive atmosphere helped me overcome my self-doubt, and although Greek and Latin remained my most challenging classes, they no longer struck terror in me.

I came into my MA planning to do a major research paper (MRP) on archaeology of the cult of Asclepius (the Greek god of healing), but that changed in my first semester. I was taking a required course on gender and sexuality in ancient Greece, which was not a topic I had ever thought about studying. It turned out to be one of those courses that changes the way you look at the entire world. By studying gender roles and ideas of sexuality in the ancient world, I started paying attention to gender roles and sexuality in the modern world, too. I started to think critically about social justice issues that I had always taken for granted before as "just the way things are." Rather than approach ancient medicine through its connection to religion, I stumbled across the possibility of approaching ancient medicine through gender roles. I began to wonder how ancient ideas and fears about gender roles influenced who was "allowed" to practice medicine, and how their practice was viewed. With the encouragement of my professor and mentor, Dr. Allison Glazebrook, my research paper for that course eventually evolved into my MA thesis, "Gender and Healing in the Hippocratic Corpus."

The idea of doing a thesis was somewhat daunting. But it was precisely because of that that I was eager to embrace the challenge, and I'm very glad I did. Most students in my program do an MRP that is much shorter than a thesis and doesn't require an oral defense. The idea of not only writing a thesis of over a hundred pages, but then having to stand up and defend it orally was scary, but I was confident I could do it with the support of my supervisor and that it would be good practice for my future PhD. It was definitely a worthwhile experience—I had an exciting research area that could carry me into a PhD, and I learned so much about the process of working with a committee and how to tackle a huge writing project.

One of the biggest things I learned through this was the value of letting go of my own writing. By working with my supervisor and committee and seeing them as allies negotiating the research and writing process, I learned to trust them to help make my work the best it could be, not just for my sake, but for theirs and the program's, too. Learning to trust others with my writing in a collaborative sense continues to pay off in my writing. In my current work, for example, I do a lot of short writing of news articles, which are then sent to an editor before being published by the university. While I do the best writing job I can, I also know that it's not going to be perfect. I have no qualms in trusting the editorial team to make my writing better. When I am working on large writing projects, I think of it in term of a thesis, breaking it down into smaller chapters and then chunks within that. Research is just as important to my writing now as it was to my thesis—I have a responsibility to communicate other people's academic work in an accurate and accessible manner. Writing is a very personal thing, but as one instructor I know says, "Writing is something we do, not something we are." By sharing my work with others and being open to feedback, I continue to become a stronger writer.

One of my most valuable experiences during graduate school was being involved in the university beyond my department and program. Our university has a Graduate Students' Association (GSA), a student union for graduate students, and I represented our program on their council, then went on to help out as vice president of communications. Little did I know at the time that this would be the start of my social media work. Connecting with students in diverse programs enriched my own academic experience. I could see how different the graduate student experience was across the university. I was also able to advocate for the needs of humanities graduate students and, drawing on my own experience as well, raise issues affecting graduate students with disabilities. My involvement in the GSA over two years introduced me to the variety of academic subjects, methods, and cultures that exist across the university.

I discovered my passion for teaching during my MA, and took full advantage of the teaching assistant training program offered by the university's Centre for Pedagogical Innovation. While completing these workshops was entirely voluntary, it was worthwhile use of my energy. I found a group of like-minded people from across the university who cared about pedagogy and their students. My own teaching improved dramatically, and with the support of my supervising professors, I experimented with various techniques in my seminar. The workshops also encouraged me to think reflectively about what I do and why I do it, and that is something that I continue with today. I enjoy working with students immensely—they are smart, talented, funny, and inspiring people, and by the end of each semester I find I am reluctant to say goodbye to them.

Taking advantage of these opportunities to get out of my program "silo" helped me understand academia more widely and encouraged my sense of curiosity beyond my own discipline. It also helped me establish a network of friends and acquaintances. When the time came that I was finished with my MA and looking for work, I had people that knew me and, in some cases, could help me find opportunities.

The Decision: Changing Paths

The decision to leave academia after my MA was not an easy one. I had spent eleven years in postsecondary education. I had left the beginnings of a full-time career to complete a second degree. I had poured blood, sweat, and tears into learning two ancient languages (ok, maybe not blood, but definitely sweat and tears!). I had given up full-time work and the chance to build a career to pursue my dream of a PhD. The thought of leaving was like staring into a bottomless, black pit. Who would I be without my academic identity?

I distinctly remember the crisis moment for me, when I questioned my place in my chosen field. As I've said above, while I enjoyed studying language and puzzling out translations, I was not gifted in this area. Memorization was a struggle, as was concentration and focus at times due to my disability. I was not in classics for philology; rather, for me, I needed to master the languages so I could study what I really wanted—social history of ancient Greece.

It was, unfortunately, a Latin course that proved to be my final straw. I knew how much work I was putting into my translations, but I was consistently stuck at the same grade and not seeing improvement. I couldn't understand what I was doing wrong—I couldn't identify what it was I didn't know. The advice I received from professors was just to do more translation, but I struggled to see how doing more would help if I didn't understand what was tripping me up and causing me to keep making the same mistakes.

I went home after that meeting with a sense of despair. I felt I was staring into an abyss. If I couldn't hack a fourth-year Latin course, how would I ever get through a PhD? I was struggling so much with memorization—was I just dense or was it my disability working against me? How could I ever find my way around that? Had I come to the end of my ability?

I didn't pull the plug on my academic dreams immediately. I loved classics, I loved researching, and I really loved teaching. I had invested so much in it, and I wanted to find a way to make it work. I had found a research niche with my MA thesis work on ancient medicine that would lead naturally into a PhD topic. I had become increasingly interested in modern reception of Greek ideas about health and disease and how these influenced the development of modern medicine. I was also interested in the use of Greek mythology in the history of art and literature, right up to our modern-day stories. So, while I continued to wrestle with ancient languages and consider whether I had reached the end of my ability, I also started considering PhD programs in related fields.

Of course, I did decide eventually to forgo the PhD and the academic track all together. I made an attempt at one PhD application just in case, but I didn't get into the program and found that I wasn't that upset about it. I didn't know what I was going to do, but I did know I wasn't going to be working toward a PhD (yet).

There were quite a few factors that went into my decision to leave academia, but I think it mostly boiled down to time and disability.

I had already spent eleven or twelve years in academia. My second BA, which in theory should have taken two years, took me three and a bit on account of not being able to manage a full course load. Likewise, my two-year MA took me three to finish. While on paper a PhD would be four years, an average completion time of seven to nine years was often possible. When I started my MA I was already older than most, and by my calculations I would be lucky to complete my PhD by age forty. Given the oversupply of qualified candidates for full-time, tenure-track positions in my field, I could easily envision spending close to a decade crisscrossing the continent following contract work. That sounded exhausting and unsustainable. And if I left academia after a PhD, I would be nearly ten years older and in the same position as I was when I finished my MA. Would I still be able to get what I wanted out of life if I spent another decade chasing something that might not happen anyway?

To be clear, I do not believe that age determines what one can or can't do. But I also felt I had to be realistic about what I wanted out of life, and I did want to establish a career of some sort at some point. PhD programs aren't going anywhere, so did I need to do it right now? Or could I do some of the other things I wanted in life—putting down some roots, seeking (relatively) secure employment, focusing on family and loved ones and my long-neglected hobbies—and return to academia for its own sake later, perhaps as a retirement project rather than a career choice?

The second significant factor was my disability. Having a chronic, invisible illness is a big part of my life, and living with disability—in my case, chronic pain and fatigue that can fluctuate on a daily basis—takes a lot of physical, mental, and emotional energy. Graduate school demands a lot of physical, mental, and emotional energy, too. I wasn't sure that the realities of living with disability and the realities of academia were going to mesh. I didn't see or hear about disabled professors and academics in classrooms or conferences, and while my grad program had been largely supportive, I heard stories from others about how they were treated when dealing with illness or disability. This ableist atmosphere came, too, in the remarks from senior academics about other students experiencing illness or needing academic accommodations—those comments about how certain people shouldn't be in academia if they need accommodations or can't "hack it" (whatever that is supposed to mean!). I knew that while my MA experience had been supportive, there was no guarantee I would find the same in a PhD program, and in fact, there might be a very good chance that academic barriers would push me out sooner or later. I hope it's changing, and I want to believe it's changing, but to be honest, I was not ready to take on the additional work of fighting for support and recognition on top of doing a PhD and living with a disability.

I said there were two factors, but I think it's really three. The third factor was my own curiosity. Instead of narrowing my research focus, in many ways grad school opened me up to even more possibilities. There are so many diverse things I wanted to learn about from across the humanities and beyond. All the advice I had heard and read said you needed to be passionate about your topic as you started a PhD. I had lots of curiosity, but I wasn't sure if I was passionate enough about any one interest to make it through a PhD. From everyone I had talked to, everything I had read, I knew the PhD experience was really a test of how badly you wanted the PhD, and no matter how much you loved your topic, there would be times when you hated it. So not being able to focus on a singular topic of interest was another sign to me that the time was not right for a PhD.

It was a confusing decision, a scary decision, but ultimately the best decision I could have made.

Finding a New Path

Once I decided to leave academia, I had to figure out what career I wanted and how to get there. The process wasn't quick or easy. Brock University relies heavily on a system that combines weekly lectures with smaller seminars, so in a department with a smaller graduate student population, there were opportunities for nongraduate students to work as teaching assistants. While there was no guaranteed amount of work, I was fortunate to get several classes each semester. It gave me space to figure out what I wanted to do without cutting myself off from the academic community. It meant, too, that I could continue to teach and share the knowledge and skills I built up over my MA. I could still be a part of and contribute to my discipline and academic department.

I supplemented my TA contracts with other work. I started with retail and then returned to working in museums for a while. I continued to apply for any relevant jobs at my university and tried to find other local opportunities. I wanted to stay in the area for a number of reasons: the thought of moving somewhere new and starting over with finding friends, developing a support network, even finding a doctor who understood my condition, was overwhelming. Here, I was within visiting distance of my parents and my wonderful nieces, and I liked being close to so much nature in Niagara. This decision probably did make it harder to find work, but it also meant I didn't have to uproot my life.

The most frustrating thing about trying to find a job post academia was being simultaneously over- and underqualified. My experience, and that of my friends, was that employers saw someone with an MA as overqualified and, therefore, a flight risk. At the same time, not having a college diploma was an underqualification—many employers wanted someone who was already trained for the job.[1] It is a very difficult position to be in, and while I did get help from my university's career services to frame my academic experience as work experience, I looked into obtaining additional qualifications from a community college. Having spent twelve years studying, though, I was reluctant to commit to a full-time two-year college program.

One avenue I considered was working in human resources. I knew I enjoyed teaching, and I was interested in how this could translate into work that involves training people. I began online courses toward human resources certification, but when I found after the second course that the content still wasn't engaging me, I suspended that effort.

After briefly also contemplating a career in editing, I went back to museum work. I enjoyed the exhibition research projects and working my way through archival material as well as transcribing century-old letters and documentation. Although I liked thinking about how the research could be communicated through visual display, there was little room for advancement, and I still found leading educational programming exhausting. At any rate, that avenue ended when I was laid off after only nine months.

This series of trials and failures was discouraging at times, but it wasn't a complete waste. Like most people, I suspect, I'm not comfortable with failing. It felt awkward to tell people I was trying something, only to have it not work out, but it's an important process of finding what fits. I had the opportunity to chat with an earlier graduate of my MA program who built a successful career as a freelance archaeological illustrator, and her advice was valuable: keep trying things until something sticks. That is now the advice I pass along to students: be curious, be willing to try new things, and be willing to fail.

Unexpected Opportunities

The "something that stuck" for me was not anything I would ever have imagined: Twitter. Yes, somehow, I have managed to turn tweeting into my career path, and in a way that keeps me connected to academia.

My engagement with academic Twitter started during a first-year myth class on Greek and Roman heroes that I was TA-ing. I had been a TA for the course several times and was very familiar with the content, so when my colleague Darrin Sunstrum suggested that we do some live tweeting, it seemed like a simple decision. With the professor's permission, we tweeted during lecture using a course hashtag, which we also used to share supplemental material. I quickly saw firsthand how social media can break down the so-called ivory tower and bring the world into a classroom. While not many of the 450 students engaged openly with our tweets, we did converse with classicists from around the world. It was fascinating to see how some topics would get picked up and shared. Ancient heroes resonated with people, and we showed in our tweets how they connected with modern superheroes, art, literature, and even science.

In the summer of 2016, the dean of the faculty of humanities offered me a position taking care of the faculty's Twitter and Facebook accounts. This was a new role in the faculty, and with time it has grown into a substantial (although still part-time) job. It brings together different strands of my academic experience in a way I never would have expected. The way my MA program made me more curious about connections across the humanities, for example, is a definite asset as I find myself writing about all kinds of different work and research that is happening in the humanities. My experience working with the GSA and developing connections with people across the university turned out to be a small foretaste of what I do now. I used to think of my curiosity and diverse interests as negatives—things that were keeping me from focusing on one single thing. Now, I see curiosity as important. It helps me find and tell stories about the importance and relevance of the humanities.

My connections from Twitter have brought me to where I am today. They have led to presenting conference papers and workshops, developing a professional network, and even writing this book chapter. I pick up writing and teaching tips from other academics and use Twitter to share my own ideas and resources. I engage in conversations with academics I may never meet, and on the occasions when I do go to a conference, I look forward to meeting my Twitter people in real life.

Social media has also been a way to find a new community of like-minded people. For example, I began podcasting with Darrin. We didn't know much about how to podcast, and although the tech side of things seemed daunting, we found a welcoming, friendly community of fellow podcasters. We launched *MythTake* in April 2016. It's provided an important way of staying connected to academia, but not tied to it. Our podcast is a forum for us to explore ideas related to Greco-Roman mythology and to connect with like-minded people. We talk about passages and myths that resonate with us, and we share how popular films echo the same ideas explored in Classical mythology. While we're not doing traditional scholarship, we are still engaged with scholarship and with communicating the importance of our chosen discipline in today's culture. Our episodes are peer-reviewed by hundreds of listeners, who also share their ideas and thoughts with us. We have had the opportunity to meet and record with fellow podcasters and have formed some lasting friendships.

My work in social media and podcasting has also brought me into meaningful, long-term discussions about public-facing scholarship, in classics specifically and in humanities more generally. If our discipline is to thrive, it's important that people understand what we do and why it matters. How is it relevant to people today? Why should they care about the survival of humanities programs at universities and colleges? I first saw these conversations happening on Twitter in the science community, and I was excited to find them happening in humanities, too. Scientists refer to the work of connecting the public with scientific research as sci-com; I want to be doing humanities communication, connecting people with the important work being done in the humanities. Humanities is here, it matters, and there is so much important work being done in our field.

I'm still just starting out on this career path, but I have been asked to speak and write about leveraging the power of social media to connect people with academic work. I do workshops with undergraduate and graduate students to talk about how they can use social media to continue contributing to their discipline after graduation. We need graduates to be part of that ongoing public conversation so they can introduce others to our disciplines and keep the conversations about their importance and relevance going. I'm excited to be a part of this conversation, and I'm excited to see where it goes.

Finding a New Identity

Before I close, I want to revisit the idea of identity that I brought up earlier. The loss of my traditional academic identity was something I wasn't really prepared for or sure how to navigate.

Grad school is like that expanding construction foam. It will fill up every single millimeter of your life that you allow it to, and then will demand more. There is always something more to read, more to write, and there is definitely always more translation work. There are classes—but also conferences, symposia, department talks, public lectures. No matter how enjoyable or interesting these individual events are, all these things put together demand a huge amount of physical and mental energy.

After a near burnout halfway through my first semester of grad school, when academic demands came up against my physical reality, I knew I was going to have to take control and set my own boundaries. I took a day off each week (usually Sunday) to either rest or do something just for me. And although I made a determined effort to carve out "me time," it was difficult to do and I often felt guilty that I wasn't doing more academic work instead of relaxing. I knew, though, that if I didn't take a day to physically rest and take care of my own physical, mental, and emotional well-being, I wasn't going to finish my degree.

Even with this concerted effort, many of my hobbies and interests fell to the side. As the end of grad school approached, keeping a list of all the things I looked forward to doing again kept me motivated through the final leg of my thesis. Rediscovering old interests and exploring new ones became an important part of my post-MA recovery phase.

I think grad school is such an all-consuming experience that it's easy to lose your sense of self, and there is a certain sense of loss that comes with the completion of such a project. My academic dream had defined my sense of self and purpose; who was I without it?

I've been having quite a few conversations about my experience with students thinking about leaving academia lately. Leaving academia was one of the most difficult decisions I have made in my life. I had watched other people make this decision, and while I like to think I respected their choices, I know now that I did not appreciate the bravery it takes. It is a courageous and difficult decision to leave academia. So much time, money, and effort has been invested in the pursuit of a degree, yet so much more investment is still required. Is it worth it? The answer isn't easy.

To those who choose to leave for a different path, I want to say this: academia, like banking or plumbing, is not for everyone, and it's ok if it's not for you. You are not a quitter if you leave. There is no shame in finding a different path that is more rewarding and better suited to you.

Your academic experience is still important and still worthwhile, and you will carry it with you as you go forward.

Your well-being, health, and happiness are more important than any degree. If your degree is not giving you that, then look for a different path. Consider what your degree is worth to you without happiness, or health.

To those who choose to stay in academia, I ask this: please think before saying things that suggest shame or failure when someone leaves your program. Others are listening and internalizing what you say. From faculty, fellow student, friend, or onlooker, comments that suggest it is the leaver's "fault" they "couldn't make it" contribute to an unhealthy culture. Framing this difficult decision to leave as an individual's personal shortcomings also obscures the role that academia as an institution plays in that decision. The system is far from perfect, and many good scholars with excellent ideas get forced out or flee from toxic departments before they can realize their goals. Academia needs the people who leave as much as it needs the people who stay.

I applaud those of us who take the brave and scary step to leave the traditional academic route and be independent scholars. At the end of the day, we only get one shot at life, so make sure you're living the life you want. Yes, it is hard. When you struggle with finding your identity, your purpose, your community outside of academia, know that you are not alone. There are many of us alongside you, making valuable contributions to our communities. Leaving doesn't mean you don't care about your field or discipline. It doesn't mean you can't find ways to still contribute if you wish.

Leaving is an option, not a failure.

NOTES

1. In Canada, college and university are two different systems. The college system focuses more on job and skill training, whereas the universities award academic degrees. It is not unusual to find joint college-university programs, which allow students to obtain both a university degree and a college diploma simultaneously, or for students to pursue a college diploma after completing their university degree.

2

In the Borderland: Navigating between Community College and Dual-Credit High School

JOSHUA HEVERT

I can't remember ever wanting anything so much. I was sitting at an El Paso Chihuahua's game with my wife and friends, poring over what I might be asked in an interview I had scheduled for the following day. When I finished my dissertation in May 2016, I had high hopes for the academic job market. I had written what I believed to be a decent dissertation, won an award for teaching, and served on several different committees for the history department. Although I knew that the job market was bad, I did not understand how catastrophically bad it was and is, and being offered a tenure-track job at a four-year college or university had been my goal ever since committing to graduate school. Ultimately, I figured I had done my part during graduate school and put my best foot forward, only to learn firsthand that my best foot was not enough for the ten or so tenure-track positions for which I applied that year.

Despite having earned a PhD at the University of North Carolina at Chapel Hill and having prepared for the traditional academic job market, I found myself preparing to interview for a position at

Cotton Valley Early College High School in a small rural district outside of the city of El Paso in an agricultural town called Fabens. At that point, I had never sat for an academic interview, and I was unsure what to expect when I walked into the room the next day. I only had a small amount of teaching experience, having spent the year after graduation as an adjunct at El Paso Community College. Despite this, and my knowing next to nothing about the challenges of working in an underfunded rural district with a large population of at-risk students, the hiring committee granted me the opportunity to work at the school teaching dual-credit US history and pre-AP world history. Once the district's human resources department called with the formal job offer, I very quickly accepted the position. I would learn later that two of my colleagues from the community college who were on the hiring committee helped push for the school's decision to name me the finalist.

At the time, I had absolutely no idea how challenging the job was that I had just agreed to undertake. Nor did I realize just how unprepared I was to teach at the high school level, especially with a group of students whose own challenges I had never knowingly confronted during my graduate preparation. I always knew that I wanted to teach, and this position seemed like the perfect opportunity for me to be in the field that I love so much and gain some experience that would help if I wanted to apply for a tenure-track job at El Paso Community College in the future. When I accepted the job at the early college, however, I knew that my relationship with academia writ large had changed. Despite rationalizing my new position as a temporary exile or pure financial survival, I felt immediately disconnected from the life I had planned out so meticulously when I started graduate school, and I wondered if I would ever be allowed to be a part of the academy again. Now an independent scholar, I have struggled to define what exactly that label means to me, someone who walks a strange line between academia and the world of kindergarten through grade twelve education. I have always understood "independent scholar" to mean someone detached from an institution of learning. However, I am attached to an institution of learning and am teaching at the college level. In this chapter, I hope that my reflection on my journey over the past three years helps mitigate the fears of someone who might choose to pursue teaching in secondary education. I have found my position quite rewarding and, generally, have found that I am still able to keep an active relationship with academia despite my "independent" status.

When I graduated from UNC, I did make an honest try at the standard academic job market. I felt the constant pull between pursuing academia wherever it led me and living the life that I had begun to cultivate for myself over the past several years. My first year on the market, there were only a handful of tenure-track positions open across the United States for a medieval historian, and even fewer that were seeking my specialty. Moreover, I am married to an academic historian who secured a tenure-track position two years prior to my completion of the doctorate. For those two years, plus an additional year during her prior position as a visiting associate professor at the University of Hawaii at Hilo, we had lived apart. I had been encouraged to stay near UNC while I finished the degree, and my funding was tied to a teaching assistantship. Aside from the financial strictures and the encouragement to stay in Chapel Hill, my partner and I had come to an agreement. Whichever one of us secured a tenure-track job first would decide where we put down our roots, unless the other one landed a better tenure-track job later. Living in separate cities, we agreed, could not be a long-term arrangement if we were going to stay married. During my time in graduate school, my partner and I met several colleagues, both graduate student and faculty, who also had to "commute" for their relationship. Some of them had shorter distances to travel, for instance, between Chapel Hill and Boston or Chapel Hill and New York, but we never envied their having to budget time and funding to make those trips just to enjoy each other's company, not to mention their having to pay for and maintain two households in separate states. It was not a future to which we would submit ourselves, even if it meant sacrificing some of our academic goals. Survival was and will always be more important to us than our scholarship; I imagine many other academic couples feel the same way.

My partner got a tenure-track job first. She landed a position at El Paso Community College (EPCC); it was a great fit for her, and El Paso, despite many (uninformed) opinions stating otherwise, turned out to be a great place to live. So, when I was done with my degree and had no position of my own, I moved to El Paso to rejoin our household. Our dog was certainly excited about this, though it left a lot of questions for me as to what precisely I would do when I got there. Of course, my partner securing a tenure-track job meant that I had new constraints on my own career opportunities. As we have spoken about several times, these limits made me, at times, feel "less than," like I was always playing career catch-up, though I never resented my partner for her success. After all, I benefited, too, since I would have an institution at which to teach in an adjunct capacity if the traditional market did not work out. At the back of my mind, I have always wondered if I could have tried a bit harder to work the market. After three years of marriage and not living together, I desperately wanted to be with my partner full time again. Perhaps, subconsciously, I did not put my full efforts into my job materials, knowing full well that if I got an offer, it would mean chaos for my marriage and potential future family.

One challenge was that the degree I earned in medieval history did not necessarily fit with the course offerings at my partner's institution. Since it is a community college, course offerings are mainly two survey sequences: the US history survey and a world history survey. My training certainly made me capable of teaching a course on world history to 1500, but since that course is not required as a part of a degree plan outside of history, its sections rarely fill to capacity, despite few sections being offered. The bread and butter of the EPCC history discipline, then, is the US history course, a specialization in which I had not taken a course since high school. However, knowing that it was likely that I would end up in El Paso, I made sure to angle for a teaching assistantship for a US history survey at UNC. Fortunately, I happened to obtain such an assignment in my final semester of working as a teaching assistant there.

Thus, my first real investment in compromising in my career for the sake of my marriage was learning a completely different area of history and trying to digest a small fraction of its historiography. EPCC had an open spot for a summer section of US history to 1877 and gave me a shot at teaching it. That first section of US history, taught in just five weeks, was quite the rough start, especially since I had not previously experienced being the official instructor of record. I had written a syllabus, designed some assessments, and had some ideas for class activities, but nothing I did at UNC could have prepared me for what I encountered once I started teaching the class. Many of my students had significant gaps in their reading and writing abilities, often connected to their status as English learners. Some of them had never heard of or seen a primary source over the course of their education, or at least were not clear about the difference between primary and secondary sources. As a result, I had to significantly change my approach; with just five weeks to get through the whole of US history to 1877, this was a monumental task to undertake. On the fly, I learned how to scaffold primary sources and lecture arguments for my students: I had to give more explicit instructions for discussion activities, and I had to walk them through building and expanding an academic argument.

Some of the training I received during my graduate experience helped me navigate this maze of new challenges, but a lot of what I had to do that summer was stumble through from class session to class session, fail to execute exactly what I planned to do in class, drag myself back to the adjunct office, and reflect on what I could do next time that might be an improvement.

Reflecting on this first attempt at teaching, I have realized that my graduate school training did little to prepare me for the rigors of teaching as the instructor of record. At the University of Hawaii and UNC Chapel Hill, I was quite fortunate in my teaching assistant assignments. Nearly without exception, my supervisors lectured dynamically, captured the students' imaginations, and inspired a great deal of critical thinking in the written assignments the instructors assigned their students to complete. But for a student teacher (which is exactly what a teaching assistant is), this is woefully inadequate preparation. Generally speaking, this leaves teaching assistants relatively on their own to learn how to teach disciplinary literacy or effective writing, and—above all else, as I learned—how to meet the needs of diverse learners in the classroom. The reality is that the vast majority of those who are able to secure tenure-track or full-time positions will be saddled with a four-four or five-five load and classes full of students who require scaffolding for most writing assignments. Indeed, even those fortunate enough to secure a tenure-track position at a top-tier university still need to have the pedagogical skills to be effective teachers in the classroom.

UNC Chapel Hill's history program offered only one seminar dedicated to pedagogy. In fact, that seminar was one of the deciding factors for me as I chose between a few PhD program offers; the other programs, at the time at least, did not offer such a seminar. A professor with a reputation for innovative and effective teaching led the seminar, and my fellow students and I took a lot of good information and ideas from our seminar meetings. Especially when it came to learning about innovative ways to incorporate technology into the classroom, the seminar was quite strong. Missing from the seminar, however, was a frank discussion about the relationship(s) between instruction and assessment, how to incorporate strong active learning strategies in the classroom, and how to navigate the more bureaucratic aspects of teaching, whether measuring student learning outcomes (SLOs) or collecting other assessment data. Without a doubt, the experience of creating a syllabus and formulating assessment ideas beyond the standard essay or exam was helpful, but a more robust discussion around the above issues would have added even more value to the pedagogy seminar.

Graduate students who want to pursue or who are thinking about pursuing teaching as their primary responsibility would be best served by networking with their university's education department. Now that I have been the instructor of record at both a community college and an early college high school, I very much wish I had followed my inclination to take or audit a course at UNC's School of Education. What caused my hesitation and eventual decision to abstain from following through on my idea was a general feeling that it would not be looked at favorably by my adviser or my department. To my adviser's credit, I was generally encouraged to follow a number of paths and diversify my experience, but I had a nagging feeling in the back of my mind that taking a course outside of my field of study, especially once I went "all but dissertation," would be a bridge too far. But now, knowing the amount of preparation that goes into lesson planning, the design of assessments, and the delivery of effective instruction, I know I would have benefited from learning about such things from experts in their fields before taking on the responsibility of the instructor of record, especially in a secondary-level classroom. At the very least, coming in equipped with some theoretical knowledge of classroom management, secondary-level pedagogy, and effective assessment design would have significantly curbed the high levels of anxiety that I felt during the days that immediately preceded the first day of school and my first "real" day in the classroom.

I survived that first five-week summer semester and had the opportunity to teach more classes in the following fall and spring as an adjunct at El Paso Community College. As many PhD graduates know, the life of an adjunct instructor comes with a sense of severe financial insecurity, feelings of worthlessness, and anxiety about what the future holds. It is not a sustainable way of living. While I am fortunate to have a partner who has secured a full-time, tenure-track position, my status as an adjunct stood in the way of many of our personal goals, especially our shared financial goals. A tenure-track position opened in the fall of the first year I taught at EPCC. I applied and did not even make the interview cut. In hindsight, the reasons for this are clear: I had little experience teaching at the community college, especially online, I wrote a cover letter too focused on research and not enough on teaching, and I had yet to teach anything besides the first half of the US history survey. To make matters worse, neither my colleagues at the community college nor the college itself told me that I had not made the interview stage; I only found out when a colleague from another campus appeared in the adjunct office of my home campus and was cagey when I asked him what he was doing in that part of town. That rejection was heart-wrenching, especially as it meant another year of adjuncting and the insecurity, both emotional and financial, that came with it. I felt completely dislocated and lost, as though my training and knowledge and skills meant nothing. It sent me into a spiral of self-loathing that led me to seek out therapy in order to cope with all that the rejection meant. I often thought that my compromise had cost me my career.

If I was to have an academic career, I eventually realized, I would have to adjust my expectations for what pursuing a career in teaching history looked like. A few weeks after learning of my rejection, another colleague sent out an email to the adjuncts at our campus to inform us of an opportunity for a full-time position at an early college high school just a fifteen-minute drive from one of the campuses at which I was teaching. At first, I balked at the prospect of teaching high school. I told myself things like "That's not what I got a PhD to do"; "I cannot handle teaching teenagers"; and "Teachers have exhausting workdays. I do not think I want that for myself." Those were the things I allowed myself to say out loud. In all honesty, one thing I kept returning to in my most private of thoughts was that my degree entitled me to more, that this position was far beneath my station as someone who held a PhD from a top-tier university. My graduate student peers had landed jobs at places like the University of Iowa, Texas A&M, SUNY, and the College of Charleston. Certainly, I deserved a job like that, too. And so, at times, I told myself and my partner that I would not apply for this position. I, my pride and vanity told me, would not fall into this "lesser" position. I would not enter a separate, lower class of academics.

My partner, however, insisted that I apply. I eventually relented, realizing that the position would, as she argued, give me great teaching experience that could translate to a position with the college later and allow us to pursue some of our financial goals at a quicker pace. Plus, the position was for the early college high school, and I would be teaching dual-credit classes. So, ultimately, I would be doing the same job but at a higher volume and for a different audience. The reality ended up being much different, but these points gave me enough reason to see the application through.

The application process was straightforward. The interview, however, was not what I expected. The panel consisted of nine people, some from the early college itself, as well as the dean and coordinator of the history division from the supervising community college campus. When I was brought in, they told me that I had twenty minutes to answer the battery of questions they had posted on the desk at which they sat me. There was not a teaching demonstration, nor was there time for me to pose too many of my own questions about the campus, the position, and some of the other responsibilities that might be required of me.

What did come out of the interview was a better understanding of what an early college high school aimed to accomplish. In the brief question and answer period, several of the staff members on the committee reiterated that the school did not necessarily exist for the best and brightest in the community. Instead, the mission of the early college was to provide those who might not otherwise go to college the chance to earn an associate's degree while still in high school. At Cotton Valley Early College around 80 percent of the students who enrolled achieved their degree, and many of them had their degree in hand before they finished their high school requirements. Some of the program's students went on to receive a bachelor's degree from the University of Texas at El Paso at nineteen and were working in their fields right after they graduated; all of this was despite the challenges some of them faced, whether crushing poverty, being an English as a second language learner, or general anxiety about their status as an undocumented person. I left the room thinking about how wonderful working at such a place could be, and my vision of Cotton Valley as a last resort for full-time employment changed to seeing it as a genuine opportunity to test my teaching abilities and do some real good for this small rural community. I desperately hoped for a call back. I did not have to wait long. The district's human resources department called me a day or two later and told me that the committee had selected me for the position, but that the school board would need to approve a district-wide initiative to make my hiring official.

The initiative in question was Fabens Independent School

District becoming what the state of Texas terms a "District of Innovation." This designation allows districts to apply for certain exemptions or additions in order to accommodate students or to provide students with more opportunities. In Fabens, the district's innovation plan included the ability to hire teachers for dual-credit classes even if they did not hold a standard Texas teacher's license, as long as they had been credentialed by El Paso Community College. At the time of my interview, the school board had not yet formally approved the innovation plan. Human resources, however, assured me that the vote was likely to be in favor of the plan and that I would receive a call when it did.

It took another month, but the phone call came just days after I returned to UNC for my doctoral hooding ceremony. I had already told my PhD adviser about the position over email, but I was quite nervous about talking to him in person. My fear was that, since I was his first student to graduate, my "alternative" path would somehow disappoint him or, at worst, make him write me off as a failure. As a result, I couched my explanation of the job in ways that would seem appealing to a traditional academic. I spoke about how I would still seek to transform my dissertation into a monograph, about how I would still attend conferences regularly, and how I would be proposing course additions to the catalogue at the community college in an attempt to stay in the field. I wanted to present myself as a continuing scholar who had a different kind of job and to still feel accepted as a part of the academic "club."

Despite my fears, we had an excellent conversation about the potential trajectory of my career, how the position dove-tailed with my passion for teaching, and the sort of opportunities my students would now have because they had an instructor with a PhD in the field in the room with them. I left that conversation feeling empowered, focused, and excited for the school year to start. My partner, my family, and my friends all expressed their genuine excitement for me. Certainly, my graduate student friends shared in my relief that I had found full-time employment, and my parents expressed their pride in my accepting a job outside of my original plans. My partner expressed relief, too, since it meant that she would no longer have to shoulder most of our bills on her own.

I learned very quickly that teaching in a secondary school was not for the faint of heart nor for a lower class of academic. That August, I reported to my new campus for two weeks of orientation, professional development, and team building. Whatever excitement I had felt about the position quickly turned into anxiety. First, my principal explained my course load: I was going to be teaching dual-credit US history as expected, but I was also assigned to teach high school–level world history. My dual-credit US history sections were what my principal called "stacked," meaning that there would be students in that section of US history who would be regularly enrolled, not dual-credit, high school students. It was not completely clear to me if these "stacked" classes meant I needed to prepare and execute two lesson plans for the same class period or if I could run things the same way. Even more frustrating was the fact that the junior-level US history course in Texas only covers from 1877 to the present, whereas the students enrolled in dual-credit were about to take a semester-long survey of US history to 1877. All of this combined with a veritable soup of other unexpected circumstances that made my head spin: I would be teaching seven classes, I had to learn about special education accommodations, I would have students who had only an elementary understanding of English, and I would be responsible for shepherding the US history students through their state-level US history exam at the end of the year.

I immediately realized that the plans I had made for the course over the summer needed significant revision. That made taking on other responsibilities, particularly the two courses I had agreed to teach for EPCC to make some extra money to pay down debt from student loans and credit cards, seem nearly insurmountable. I had the first of a handful of severe panic attacks just a few days into the faculty development period. I had never taught so many classes before. I worried that I would be unable to connect with my students. The imposter syndrome that plagued me during graduate school came rushing back and had me questioning why the district decided to waste a chance on me when there were other, probably more qualified candidates for the job—ironic since I myself had looked down my nose at the position just a few months before. Moreover, the trainings that the district held for our professional development only deepened these anxieties. There were terms and acronyms—GT, EL, IEP, 504—about which I had only vague knowledge. Some of the trainings made teaching seem like an alien profession with which I had only a passing familiarity. I was assured I would be fine, that these were just the usual first-year jitters and I would find a way to capture my students' attention. A fellow teacher even handed me a book, *The Fundamental 5: The Formula for Quality Instruction*; another gave me *The First Days of School*. I took them home and read them; I tried researching high school–level lesson plans and started making PowerPoints just to focus my nervous energy into something. I was a wreck.

The breaking point came during the second week of professional development when I was introduced to the Texas state teacher appraisal system, T-TESS (Texas Teacher Evaluation and Support System). Learning this new system proved to me once and for all that I had to relearn how to teach and that I needed to do it quickly. During the previous year, I had become used to the standard student evaluations and to having one of the campus history coordinators observe one class and walk me through the evaluation process. While El Paso Community College does many things very well, its teacher appraisal system lacks a great deal and relies on the seriousness of the evaluator to be anywhere near effective. The evaluation often feels like a formality and offers little in the way of constructive criticism to help push the instructor's teaching practice forward. T-TESS, on the other hand, requires a deep engagement on the part of the principal and/or other evaluators, evidence of teaching practice, and a deep reflection from the teacher at the end of the process. It has detailed criteria for what an effective teacher does in the classroom and the sort of professional activities in which a teacher should be participating. At the bottom of the T-TESS rubric sits a continuum that runs from "student-centered" to "teacher-centered." As a teacher does more "student-centered" instruction and activities, the teacher's appraisal rating increases. As a community college instructor, I had relied a lot on lecture and knew only a few active learning strategies. I thought I was screwed; surely my lack of teaching ability would be exposed as soon as I had students in my room. I had another panic attack. There were many, many tears. A few of my new coworkers became convinced that I would not be back when I had to leave early one day.

Over the next several weeks, I began to get the rhythm of teaching at the early college. I made it through the first week by doing some team building and introductions with my students. I started introducing the course material with lecture format but began to transition to more active learning techniques. I learned how to balance the rigors of "bell-to-bell" instruction with the massive amounts of grading and planning required for each week. While my anxiety remained at a peak, I would sit with my partner at our dining room table and talk through a week of planning, and she would walk me through different strategies she had tried. I kept researching best practices when I had the time. Eventually, it clicked. I became more confident in my lesson planning, my classroom instruction got better slowly, and I managed to connect with my students, even if it took a while. I even picked up a bit of Spanish as I listened to my students talk with each other in my classroom. But still, at the back of my mind, I felt as if I was missing a few critical components of a teacher's toolbox, and some of the activities my partner and I planned began to feel a bit stale after a few weeks. Then, however, I started working toward a Texas teacher's certificate, and it was my experience in an alternative certification program that opened my eyes to what teaching in the secondary classroom really entailed.

The admissions process for the certification program was somewhat grueling. The first step in the process required passing the certification test (TExES, the Texas equivalent of the Praxis exam) for the content area for which I was applying. I decided to take on the composite social studies certification because it was much more marketable than a history-only certification. Studying for a certification test, admittedly, felt insulting. Because I had a PhD in the field, I often felt I should be exempt from having to take the exam. Especially after taking and passing PhD exams in graduate school, another test felt like much too much of a burden. The test also cost $150 to take, and I had to spend additional money on preparation materials for the fields of social studies in which I had no real experience, particularly economics.

Beyond the foundational knowledge that the program provided, completing my certification yielded two significant consequences. The first was that I discovered just how much interest I have in teaching historical literacy explicitly. After working at the literacy clinic over several summers, explicit instruction in literacy had become one of my primary areas of interest when it came to pedagogy. The second positive consequence of completing the alternative certification program was that I was able to build a significant network with other educators in the El Paso area, including many of my mentors. While much of this network provided a means for moral support throughout the year I was in the program, it also opened many doors for professional opportunities. As part of the alternative certification program, the facilitators conducted five visits to observe a lesson that the intern had prepared. After the first observation, the program gave me the option to have my second filmed so that we could break down the lesson segment by segment to highlight my specific strengths and weaknesses in literacy instruction. I agreed, despite feeling a great deal of nervousness about the process. But, ultimately, I was glad to have done it. The lesson went very well and the program now uses it to help demonstrate how other social studies instructors can incorporate literacy instruction into their lesson plans. Without the encouragement of the program, I probably would not have taken a leap of faith and had my teaching documented and broken down to its fundamentals. Now, I encourage other instructors, whether at the early college or at the community college, to take the same risk to push their practice forward. Doing so thrust me into an instructional leadership role on my campus, which has me at the forefront of our professional development programs. I've also been able to take a lot of what I learned from the alternative certification program into my college classroom, and my teaching has improved in countless ways.

The amount of time I have had to dedicate to becoming an effective classroom teacher has come with sacrifice, of course. I have had to make several adjustments to my long-term goals and my relationship to the academy. My greatest loss has been in my research in medieval history; I had to deprioritize that to keep up with the burdens of teaching at the secondary level and maintaining a presence at the community college, in hopes of maybe securing a tenure-track job there in the future. On the other hand, my journey through the rigors of secondary education, and especially the alternative certification, has given me a new appreciation for pedagogy and developing methods of teaching history that work at several different skill levels. I have discovered the interest and passion I have for teaching literacy in a history classroom and developing practical exercises to further students' abilities in our discipline. I do cherish this freedom and know that I would not enjoy the same sort of intellectual flexibility if I had been able to obtain a traditional tenure-track position at a university. And, if I am completely honest, I think I have more to contribute to the pedagogical side of the historical enterprise than I ever did as a researcher of medieval church history.

That is not to say, however, that I have completely stopped trying to maintain an active presence within my field of medieval history; however, the way in which I engage with the field has had to change considerably, mostly due to a loss of resources. I have lost, for example, the wealth of resources available to me through the UNC library, especially access to JSTOR, since EPCC does not currently have a subscription to the service. I am able to do some research through the library at the University of Texas at El Paso, but the library grants me only the same privileges as a community member, not a scholar of the university, nor do they offer a visiting scholars program for additional privileges. As a result, I have had to pay for a JPASS subscription to access journal articles and buy monographs that my campus library does not have in its holdings and does not have the funds to buy. My school district also does not have the funds to support conference travel, so if I want to travel to conferences I have to pay out of my own pocket.

In the time I have held my current position, I have been able to travel to one conference, the 2018 International Congress on Medieval Studies (ICMS) at Kalamazoo, Michigan. Notably, it was my attendance at this conference that made me feel the most "separated" from my field, even though I was in its epicenter. When I submitted my abstract in response to the call for papers, I put the community college as my institution. But when I formally registered for the conference after my paper and the panel of which it was a part had been accepted, I listed the early college instead, and that is what appeared on my conference badge. My decision to do this came down to wanting to show my students that their small border town would be represented in this international academic space, and, dammit, I was proud to represent them there, too. My peers at ICMS hardly took notice, but I did feel divorced from the field when I entered the book fair. I distinctly remember that when I walked up to one publisher, University of Toronto Press, the representative, after seeing my badge, said that they did not really serve someone in my role, as if I were a droid trying to enter the Mos Eisley Cantina. All this really meant was that I was not entitled to an examination copy of some of their books, but it made me feel less than in a way that I had not really felt before. In addition, I was in the midst of grading and preparing for the final weeks of the semester, so I had to stay cloistered in my dorm room to work instead of being out and enjoying the conference, save for a few panels that I refused to miss.

Most of my engagement with the field comes from networking with other scholars on social media platforms, especially Twitter. In many ways, Twitter has saved me from feeling like a complete outsider. I read threads from scholars in my field about the present state of their research, I learn about calls for papers for conferences, and I see where the fault lines in the field are drawn and am able to consider on what side(s) of certain historiographical arguments I fall. I also use some of these ideas in the classroom with my students. The platform is also helpful in determining which of my peers are "safe." If I see a fellow scholar berate or bully another peer, I know not to engage with them on their feeds or to prepare myself for the sorts of responses I could get if I post a thread of my own. For an emerging scholar, yet to publish any of my own research, this is indispensable as I seek out trustworthy scholars with whom to share my work and as I prepare for harsher criticisms if I take that work to a conference.

Teaching at the secondary level, however, does not leave me much time to engage the field as much as I would prefer in the way that I would prefer. I spend most of my noninstructional time grading, researching primary sources to use in the classroom, and building lessons around those sources. Independent research and advancement occur only during the available time in the summer, and, truthfully, only in fits and starts because the rigors of the academic year take quite the mental and emotional toll. There are days that I come home from the classroom (plus teaching an evening course at the college) and just collapse on the couch and stare at the television or my phone until the clock says that it is time for me to go to bed. I find it impossible to digest a scholarly work when I am so tired that I have to rewind an episode of *The Office* that I have seen more than once to remember what happened; writing is no different. Even during the summer, the pull toward rest and recuperation pulls me away from articles and monographs or from sharpening the Latin skills I spent so long honing. None of this rest is unproductive, but it does keep me away from my research, which I find myself missing more and more.

The teaching load has also had a somewhat deleterious effect on my marriage: the emotional availability required for teaching at the secondary level, especially at a school in which the majority of the student body lives in extreme poverty, leaves me somewhat unavailable to my partner. Some of the stories that my students have told me sound like they come out of horror novels or some weird sadistic fiction; they are absolutely ghastly. Furthermore, my partner and I have had difficulty communicating about when our respective jobs have eaten our energy past the point of exhaustion. Our fights have, at times, descended into a debate about who lives the busier life: the secondary teacher who teaches college on the side or the full-time tenure-track faculty member. I do not think we will ever come to an agreement on this, either. We have recently sought couples therapy to work through these issues, but it will take time for us to recover the relationship that we enjoyed prior to me starting in my position at the early college.

None of this is to say, however, that I have become so disenfranchised from the academy that I never want to return. If a tenure-track opportunity at the community college opened, I would most certainly apply for it and accept it if it was offered to me. After all, I still feel like I am a part of the wider network of academics, even if I do not have the title of "assistant professor" on my CV. I still feel a great emotional attachment to my research and believe I have important things to say about my field. I hope that one day I will find the time to publish my work. I will certainly try to attend conferences as I can afford to do so. Most importantly, I still have the opportunity to introduce new generations of students to the wonders of the past and to try to make them fall in love with history the same way that I did. Those are all things I can do as a secondary-level teacher. I am doing the work of a scholar, even if my institution does not have the word "university" in its name and my students are under eighteen. I am not the only one. There are so many other scholars waiting in the cold outside the closely guarded gates of academia, waiting to be brought into the fold and to be recognized for the crucial work that they do in and for their fields. If academia can expand its notion of "membership," our scholarship and our students will be the better for it.

PART TWO

LEAVING THE IVORY TOWER

3

So, You Want to Teach History, but Not in a Classroom?

ALLYSON SCHETTINO

Part I

We should start, I suppose, with the fantasy, although that is by far the most embarrassing part. By which I mean we should start with what I thought graduate school, and by extension all of academia, was going to be like. This part isn't pretty, and, fair warning, gets into triggering territory fairly rapidly. But it is also the truth, and the inciting incident for all the good that has come after. So, let's get through it together, shall we?

The trouble began because I loved being an undergrad. I excelled at being an undergrad. Spending four years in an academic institution where my only job was to take as many classes as possible so I could learn as much as I could was a literal dream come true. I loved sitting in lectures, reading new books, writing papers—I even loved getting my ass handed to me from time to time, because it meant I had learned a new way to think about the world. I would spend the hours of my work-study in the library reading books on hold from other classes outside my major, as a way of learning things I couldn't possibly squeeze in to my already overextended schedule. When I applied to undergrad, I wrote in my personal essay that it was my dream to become a renaissance woman, someone who knew a little bit about everything. When I graduated, the dean read that passage from my essay aloud at the ceremony and congratulated me on achieving my goal through my rigorous coursework.

So graduate school was the holy grail of postgrad possibilities. I thought it was my ticket to nirvana. I could spend the next five to eight years continuing to do what I loved the most, and at the end of it all I could get a job where I could teach and mentor other passionate learners forever. I believed this fantasy so wholeheartedly that it is exactly what I wrote in my application essay: I wanted to get my PhD so that I could teach and inspire future generations of learners. That is how little I understood the world I was about to enter.

I was rejected from every PhD program I applied to. It was only my alma mater that took pity on me and offered me a place in their one-year master's program, provided I was willing to pay. This should have been a big red warning flag, but I barreled ahead. There were other red flags I blissfully ignored. My beloved academic advisor gently explained that her path to tenureship simply didn't exist in the world anymore. A less-beloved professor grilled me on my willingness to truly dedicate myself to one niche subject forever, before disappearing midsemester into what I can only presume was a psych ward or rehab (the school flatly refused to tell us where he had gone, and gave us all As on the course to make up for his increasingly erratic behavior).

But none of this registered. I fought tooth and nail with the school during the summer after my graduation for a scholarship to the program, and in August I won! I was headed to graduate school on a full scholarship, with a graduate assistant position thrown in for good measure. I needed to complete one year, and then I could take my accolades and my diploma and apply for a PhD program. Someday, I would be a tenured professor, living a fascinating, comfortable, and rewarding life. It was all laid out before me.

I tell you this, not because I am proud of this moment in my life, but because in the time since my stint in graduate school I've come to realize that I am not alone in having this particular idea of what graduate school and academia have to offer. If I seem to you, dear reader, to be hopelessly immature and naive at this moment in the story, please understand that I know that now. But I strongly suspect that at least a few people out there will empathize or even identify with how I felt about the possibility of a life in academia. I include this part of the story for them because I'm not sure there is nearly enough out there about what graduate school actually is. Dreamy reader, I write this for you.

It took exactly three days of graduate school orientation for my fantasy to come crashing down around my ears. The first blow was meeting my fellow graduate students, all of whom were frighteningly smart, sophisticated, and concerned with much higher goals than mere teaching. I was way out of my depth.

The second blow came at the mandatory campus counseling center orientation. A stream of exhausted, deflated graduate students in the latter years of their studies told us that there was absolutely no shame in needing to seek emotional support during graduate school. They cited frankly terrifying statistics about the rate of major depression and suicide attempts in grad programs across the country. I am no stranger to mental health struggles. I had experienced bouts of anxiety and depression serious enough to warrant counseling since the age of eight. But I had never been in a position where those conditions were just considered standard side effects of the whole experience.

The crushing blow came at the end of the third day of

orientation, when I shared a cab home with the woman who had been appointed my thesis advisor (my one-year master's program meant that I was starting my thesis immediately, with absolutely no idea how to do such a thing). I gushed to her about my areas of interest, and what I planned to write my thesis on. And she laughed. Hard. She told me my idea was absurd, and set a time where I could meet with her to form a better plan.

Three days in, and I was terrified. It only got worse from there.

You see, what I didn't understand about graduate school is that you are expected to be a fully functioning adult who already knows how to do things. And while I could read and write papers like a champ, I had no idea how to use a research library, speak extemporaneously with a small group of peers all trying to prove they are the best, write original research, or, most importantly, defend myself from the onslaught of critique that graduate school is predicated on. Four weeks in I quietly wept through an entire class because I couldn't stop but didn't feel comfortable excusing myself from the table. No one acknowledged my tears, or checked in with me after class. Probably because they didn't want to make me feel worse. But at the moment all I could assume was that I was simply weaker, unqualified, unfit to be at that table.

By six weeks in I was suicidal.

There are two things that saved my life at that critical moment. The first was my family, my boyfriend and my parents, who monitored me closely, communicated with each other constantly, and when things reached a crisis took me seriously and got me the help I needed. If you are struggling with suicidal ideation, tell someone. Tell everyone. Don't stop saying it. The people who love you will want to know, and they will want to help you.

The second thing was a comment from a professor. At my absolute nadir I begged my boyfriend to come with me to campus, so I could tell my professor that I couldn't come to class, and would probably never be back. So I could tell someone that I couldn't cut it, and have them witness my shame (major depression is a joy). But when I choked back tears and told him I wouldn't be attending that day because I thought another class would be the absolute end of me, he looked at me calmly and said he would miss hearing my thoughts on that day's reading. That was enough. Knowing one person valued my input gave me the courage to keep going. If you are struggling with suicidal ideation, tell someone. Tell everyone. Don't stop saying it. People you never could have imagined caring will care, and they will want to help you.

I got myself some serious medication, and weekly therapy, and kept grinding away at graduate school. I desperately wanted to quit, but my parents insisted I couldn't without some kind of other plan in place, and I didn't have the energy to make one, so I carried on. I hated every second of it, and I couldn't wait to be free of academia forever. But as my treatments took hold, my work improved, and I managed to graduate without shaming my advisor. To my horror, she even started laying plans for my PhD applications. I politely declined. The day I handed in my thesis and left campus forever is still one of the most liberating experiences I've ever had.

Now I just had to figure out how to survive in the real world with a master's degree in medieval history.

Part II

"I have a master's degree and no marketable skills."

This mantra, which I chanted to myself constantly, was the first hurdle I had to overcome in my postgraduate life. Since announcing my intention to major in history and English back in undergrad, a steady stream of well-meaning family and friends had cautioned me to reconsider. What, they wondered, does a person *do* with a degree in history and English? While my sights were set on academia this concern was easy to brush off. When I announced my plans to study medieval history in graduate school, there were grumbles of concern, but everyone understood that I was on a path and that there were clear steps to follow. A job, and financial stability, awaited me at the other end (I should say that absolutely none of these well-meaning friends and family were in academia themselves. They didn't know about the ongoing collapse of the job market for postdocs, and I was not foolish enough to tell them).

But now, my dreams of being a professor were over. I was out in the world with a BA in history and English, and an MA in medieval history, and absolutely no interest in becoming a teacher. I didn't want to be stuck teaching a government-appointed history curriculum. Moreover, graduate school had taught me to hate my field. I wanted to get as far away from the study and practice of history as possible. But the nagging doubt, planted by the well-meaning, remained. By all practical measures, I had no marketable skills. How would I ever convince a person to give me a job?

If you ever find yourself in the same situation, I urge you to take a step back and remember this: those well-meaning people of the world who dismiss the liberal arts as too soft and impractical are wrong. You should study whatever brings you pure joy in college, because you will never have the opportunity for unfettered, self-directed learning again. And even the most seemingly frivolous subjects, if pursued with passion, will teach you plenty of practical life skills that will make you attractive to any number of employers in any number of fields. In pursuing my degrees, I learned to process massive amounts of complex information in inhumanly short time. I learned to analyze, categorize, and store this information in a way that kept it immediately accessible at a moment's notice. I learned to easily identify what was most important in a document or book, and ignore the rest. I could write about literally anything in a manner that was engaging and persuasive, and I could hold my own in in-person debates over contested issues. I had survived an environment intended to break people down, and in the process had learned basic truths about myself, who I was and how I operated, that could no longer be shaken. And, maybe most importantly, I knew what I could not tolerate, and I knew I could get myself out of those situations.

It took me years to finally understand this, so I pass it along to you. Look past the information you've learned in the pursuit of your degree(s), and think about the skills you've acquired. Each and every one is attractive to a future employer and is increasingly rare in a world where the vast majority of undergrads are pursuing career-track degrees. The world will always need people with a liberal arts skill set. You have value!

My only goal after grad school was to find a job that could pay my bills in a field as far away from academia as I could get. Through friends I landed two jobs in quick succession. The first was booking speakers for a corporate conference firm. The company planned daylong events on topics interesting to business professionals, but no one who worked there had any particular expertise in these fields. My academic training made me a perfect fit for a job that required reading just enough about a topic (corporate IP, supply chain logistics, CX/UX) to learn who the leaders in the field were, and then contacting them to invite them to speak at our events. It was, essentially, exactly what I had done in graduate school to prepare for every seminar or guest lecture, but now I could make a salary doing it! This was my first realization that maybe graduate school wasn't a total waste after all.

After about six months I was offered more money to become an executive assistant to the chairman of a private equity firm. If you aren't familiar, which I certainly wasn't, private equity people are the folks who make huge investments in growing businesses to become the controlling partners, spend a few years getting the businesses operating at peak capacity, and then sell them at a profit. The firm was small, and all of the partners were serious business professionals with degrees from the best business schools in the country.

But the support staff, which I was joining, was made up almost entirely of people like me. The receptionist had studied Chinese literature. The office manager had worked her way up from practically nothing. This was the first time I realized one of the modern world's dirty little secrets: big businesses, STEM leaders, engineering firms, and financial institutions need people with liberal arts skill sets to keep their companies operational. We're the folks who know how to write, can comfortably chat up clients and investors, and can do the practical work that keeps businesses afloat. And they are willing to pay us big money to do it! In my first year with the company I paid off my student loans, took a trip to Paris, and banked about ten thousand dollars. My degrees had quite literally paid for themselves. Sure, it was a fraction of what the partners were making, but I didn't need that kind of money to thrive.

The trouble was that I didn't want to climb the private equity ladder, or to become a partner. I didn't want to stay in that field at all. By the end of my first year free of academia, I missed it terribly. I loved learning and teaching about history, and as much as I loved having the financial freedom my job afforded me, I couldn't get excited about the work the company was doing. This was not true of all my colleagues among the support staff. Some of them fell in love with the business, and went on to get MBAs and become quite successful in their own rights. But with a year out in the greater world, I had confirmed something I had known since I was an undergrad. History education was my passion. I just needed to find a way to do it.

My time in the world of for-profit and finance was certainly not wasted. In addition to paying off my loans, and giving myself a little nest egg, I learned how to operate in the for-profit world and how to keep people with big money happy. When I share my career story with high school and college students, they are always shocked to hear about this particular detour. But there are no wasted experiences in life. You learn something valuable everywhere you go. I now had a new skill set and the firm knowledge that no amount of money could make me happy doing something that didn't align with my interests. Those are two things well worth knowing.

Part III

We've now arrived at the second most embarrassing part of my story. I wish I could tell you that I met with trusted advisors from my time in college and graduate school, and they gave me sage advice about new avenues to explore. Or that I went to the library and did a thorough search of the field of history and stumbled upon an exciting opportunity. Or that I started attending conferences and networking events in my field, and made connections that led to new places. But we've spent some time together at this point, and I think you've come to learn a little bit about what kind of person I am. So I'll level with you.

I googled, "What do you do with a history degree that isn't classroom teaching?"

Could anything be stupider?

But, that's exactly what I did, and, gods preserve me, it worked.

Google spit back a career field I had never heard of before: museum education. Now, I should say that as I am writing this, in 2019, museum education could be said to be having a moment. All of the major universities in New York City, where I live, have started museum education master's programs that pump hundreds of graduates into the job market every year. There are professional organizations that hold museum education conferences and offer networking opportunities at workshops and meetups all year round. In short, museum education is now a recognized, viable option for people graduating from college. But when I first made my Google query, most of these things did not exist, or were very brand new. Solid information was scarce.

Which isn't to say the act of teaching in museums was new. The field was born in the early twentieth century, when the people who ran museums realized the public had no idea what to do once they got inside. Simply put, museum education is the effort to take everything in a museum—the permanent collections and the special exhibitions—and make them accessible to the general public. It is the more public-facing branch of the public history that happens in museums. But it wasn't a focus of museum leadership until 1992, when cultural institutions around the country were facing a crisis of dropping attendance. The American Association of Museums issued a report that stated that educating the public was one of the core purposes of cultural institutions generally, and should be treated as such if they wanted to survive. Even still, the most progressive institutions struggle to incorporate this principle with their other driving imperatives to collect and preserve the history and culture of humanity. But most major institutions have now accepted that if people aren't taught to appreciate the collections, they won't pay to preserve them. And so, the field of museum education continues to grow as an integral part of cultural institutions.

Based on the limited information I could find on the internet, it seemed to me that the best part of museum education was that it offered the chance to teach without being tethered to a particular set of standards. Kids would learn the basics from their classroom teachers, and I could teach them all the stuff that made history fun. It sounded like a dream job! I just had to figure out how to land it.

The first hurdle was figuring out what institutions I could

reasonably reach out to, given my background. There are about 7.8 billion cultural institutions in New York City (unofficial estimate), but a surprising few have a pure history focus. Most are art institutions of the highest order, and without any formal art history or studio art experience, I thought I was not qualified to be working at those.

And if history museums are rare in New York, *medieval* history museums are essentially nonexistent. As far as I could tell from my Google research, there were only two that had the kind of job I was looking for, and they were some of the premier institutions in the country, if not the world. The first was the Cloisters, a satellite museum of the Metropolitan Museum of Art, and one of my absolute favorite museums of all time. Landing a job there would be a literal dream come true, and was also the dream for practically every single person who wanted to work at a cultural institution. In 2008 they didn't even post jobs. You just submitted your résumé, and if at some point a job opened up and they decided you might be a good candidate, they would call you. Needless to say, I have never gotten that particular call. I did once meet a member of their education team at conference, and I'm pretty sure I terrified them with my level of excitement. I've come to accept that the Met is maybe not the institution for me.

The other medieval possibility was the Morgan Library, one of the most beautiful cultural institutions in the country. After a few years as a museum educator I did get an interview there. Reader, I panicked, and it was the absolute worst interview I've ever given in my life. The less said about it the better. Since that wretched day I've been content to admire the Morgan Library from afar.

So, with medieval options in North America beyond my reach, I turned my attention to other types of history, certain that graduate school had prepared me to cram whatever I needed to know to be able to lead tours. The New-York Historical Society was dedicated to teaching a wide swath of American history, and even better, their manager of education was willing to do an informational interview with me. So away I went.

A brief history of the New-York Historical Society is in order at this point, so you can better understand how I fell completely head over heels in love with it. The museum is the second oldest in the country, founded in 1804 by a bunch of men who had lived through the events of the American Revolution and recognized that materials relating to the nation's history needed to be preserved to start building a narrative of the American story. The institution is equal parts museum and a library, which means employees have unfettered access to both library and artifact collections. Over the years the collections were assembled according to the whims of the board of directors, so they were delightfully eclectic, with items as grand as Napoleon's authorization of the Louisiana Purchase and as mundane as cans of soup. (Not the Andy Warhol kind. Just a can of Franco-American vegetable broth from 1898. I love it.) The institution, like the city it inhabited, was hit hard by the economic downturn of the 1970s and had nearly gone under before a dedicated leadership team took the helm in the 1990s and worked diligently to save it from financial ruin.

When I visited in 2008, the New-York Historical Society had just ended a run of blockbuster exhibitions that had for the first time forced New Yorkers to confront the full history of slavery in their city, and the museum as a whole was poised for a renaissance. It was a venerable institution that had been through difficult times and was finding new footing in the world. Is it any surprise that I (over)identified with it?

And so, this is another piece of advice I offer to you, my reader. Find a place you love to be, and then do whatever it takes to be there. The rest will fall into place. I'm living proof.

My informational interview still makes me laugh whenever I

think about it. The manager was delighted with my enthusiasm, and baffled by the fact that every time he mentioned an American history scholar or debate in the field, I made a careful note in my notebook and assured him I would learn everything I could about it later. He finally blurted out, "What did you study?" and I sheepishly admitted to being a medievalist, but assured him I was going to get up to speed so I could apply for a job. "Well, why don't you just start now, and you can learn as you go?" To this day, I have no idea why he gave me a job, but I took it. And that is how I went from being a set-for-life executive assistant to a part-time museum educator making twelve dollars an hour.

Part IV

Here, in no particular order, is a list of things I've done in my ten years working in museum education:

- Cleaned vomit out of the hair of a shell-shocked fourth grader.
- Taught myself to code, and then trained an unwilling cohort of forty museum professionals so they could lead programs for children.
- Took an ambulance ride with an employee to make sure they got their workers' comp benefits on the other end.
- Counseled a twelve-year-old dealing with her parents' crumbling marriage during a museum sleepover.
- Left my home at four-thirty in the morning to try to get to a program on time (I still arrived late).
- Became a passionate advocate for teaching and learning the history of ornithology.
- Took a four-hour commute through the aftermath of Hurricane Sandy so my museum could be the only cultural institution in New York open to the public the day after the storm.

I list these things not to discourage anyone from pursuing museum education. In fact, I look back on every one of these memories with a smile. Instead, I include them to illustrate a larger point about the field in general. If you want to be a success in the field of museum education, you have to be prepared to work on anything, at any time. If someone asks you to do something, the only response should be clarifying questions. With this attitude, you'll go far.

The first pleasant surprise I encountered in my new life is that the tenets of museum education had undergone a revolution in the last twenty years. Gone were the days of "sage on the stage" style tours, where a ponderous adult led a group of uninterested children through the galleries, speaking at exhaustive length about things that could never possibly capture their attention. The teaching style at the New-York Historical Society and other institutions on the frontline of this new movement is inquiry-based instruction. Instead of telling people the facts I find most interesting, I ask what they notice about an artifact, work of art, or document, and base the conversation on their responses. The goal is never to tell a person what they need to know, but to let them use their common sense to work it out for themselves. I was their enthusiastic, encouraging guide. The hope is that by teaching people the questions to ask of the objects and images around them, we give them a skill they can use wherever they go and ignite a natural curiosity that will carry them forward into a newfound love of history.

I wasn't just sharing facts. I was helping people become historians. Exactly what I had hoped for when I first applied to graduate school!

I should take a moment to note that this inquiry strategy shares a foundation with the much better known visual thinking strategies method that has been used in art museums for years. The difference is that when you are teaching history, versus interpreting art, there are very concrete right and wrong answers. You can't let a kid look at a painting of enslaved people with smiles on their faces and draw the conclusion that slavery was a benevolent practice—that isn't just bad history, it's a travesty. The historian educator bears the responsibility of pushing students to think not just of the piece before them but also of the context in which it was made, the biases of the artist and the audience, and the value of understanding all of those things at the same time, all while making them feel that they are the masters of their own learning. In short, it is a very delicate balance. That's what makes it so fun!

The first thing I had to learn was how to help children understand why we are looking at old stuff in the first place. Students are so used to having textbooks and the entirety of the internet at their fingertips, it can be difficult for them to grasp why they would need to visit a marble hall to see a random assortment of stuff from long ago. My favorite way to begin with a particularly reticent group of students is to take the example of George Washington. We all know who George Washington is. We could, at a moment's notice, list five or six George Washington facts off the top of our head. I bet you are doing it right now. But can you name another farmer from Virginia who fought in Washington's army? Not a founding father, or a political leader, or an officer in the Continental Army. Just a regular person who became a foot soldier for a season or two, and then went back to farming.

You can't, right? Why is that? The kids are quick to tell me that this is because George Washington mattered, and this is undoubtedly true. People in his lifetime knew he mattered. They saved his papers and turned his home into a national monument. The man sat to have his portrait painted ninety-five times! But does this mean that the regular soldiers in his army didn't matter? Of course not! Washington without his soldiers spends the rest of his short life in a British prison with the rest of the Continental Congress for treason.

The history we get in textbooks is skewed toward the stories of those who made the biggest splash, but historians know that the story is much richer than that. Since we don't have dedicated libraries, national monuments, and copious painted portraits for every single person who has ever lived (yet, I quiver for my future colleagues who have to mine Twitter to make sense of our age), historians have to sift through everything that remains from past eras to learn about the lives of everyday people. And the more people we have as part of that process, with their own backgrounds, history, and contexts in which to understand the evidence, the richer the story gets.

Just as I had always dreamed, I found myself teaching the next generation of historians. But I was reaching thousands a year instead of hundreds. I felt like I had found the best job in the world.

Part V

It's taken ten years for me to climb to the position I have now. My career trajectory in the field is fairly typical, so I will try to briefly summarize it for you. Please be advised, results will vary for every individual!

A career in museum education always begins with a period my colleagues and I have fondly dubbed "the part-time hustle." Most museums have a very small staff of full-time people who oversee the department, and then a much larger contingent of part-time people who actually lead the programming with the public. A person without a trust fund usually needs two or three of these jobs to stay financially solvent—hence the hustle. These part-time positions are the entry-level positions of the field, a necessary part of the pipeline that must be endured, and I am sorry to say that given the current state of the field no amount of graduate education is going to allow one to skip it. You just have to buckle down and do it. (Important side note: internships can be part of the hustle, but most are unpaid/underpaid because the expectation is that you are receiving credit for the experience. If at all possible, just get the part-time job.)

The part-time hustle period is financially challenging (honestly, I was only able to extend mine by using the influx of gifts from my wedding to keep me afloat), but does give the dedicated hustler one huge advantage: it allows you to experience literally every aspect of the field. In my four years working part-time I led school groups, acted as a camp counselor, staffed family programs, taught professional development workshops for teachers, led adult tours, traveled for offsite programming, attended conferences and conventions as a museum representative, and helped develop various lesson plans and curricula for each of these groups. Within a few years of my personal part-time hustle, I knew exactly which parts of the job I wanted to specialize in (working with school kids!) and which parts I wanted to avoid (teacher professional development—they behave worse than their students!).

At some point during the part-time hustle, one or more institutions will grow to appreciate your particular passion, dedication, and hard work, and will take steps to ensure that you remain happily employed with them. I call this phase "permanent part-time," because you can usually give up a few of your other part-time commitments at this point and rely on a steady stream of work from one place. My permanent part-time placement came at the New-York Historical Society in my third year as an educator, when they asked me to take on regular hours to write programs and pilot a new outreach initiative they were pursuing. This is a tricky time in the career path, because it is really easy to be exploited as a permanent part-time person. You want to do everything you can to prove that you are indispensable, but you also need to make sure they know you can't stay in that position forever. Without making a huge fuss about it, during my second year as permanent part-time I let my supervisors know that my finances couldn't support being part-time very much longer. It was nothing more than the truth, and it put the ball squarely in their court. I also started applying for full-time positions all over the city, with the full support of my supervisors. That is the upside to all of this: everyone in the system has been through it before you, and they know the struggle is real. They will help you do whatever you need to make the dream happen for you.

The next step up the career ladder is the hardest to realize, because as I've already mentioned there are very few full-time positions in museum education compared to the sea of part-time employees. Unless an institution is undergoing rapid growth, or starts a new project that requires a full-time person, openings are only created when someone leaves. In my case, my direct supervisor got a prestigious new position at a different institution, and recommended me for her job. And just like that, I had made it to the other side, a full-time manager of school programs.

Making this jump is not entirely necessary. I have plenty of colleagues who have stayed at the part-time hustle or permanent part-time stages by choice for years. Some are artists who do this work to keep the lights on, some are parents who appreciate the flexibility, and some just arrived at a comfortable financial balance and feel no need to climb higher. In all honesty, I would have happily stayed permanent part-time, but I simply couldn't afford it. So up I went!

Transitioning to full-time in museum education means transitioning from being a purely public-facing deliverer of content to being someone who facilitates the logistics of making that happen. Writing programs, scheduling bookings, and training and managing the part-time staff were now my responsibility. To give you a sense of scale, the New-York Historical Society Education Department employs between forty and fifty part-time educators at any given time, and the programming serves about two hundred thousand teachers and students annually. In short, it is a lot of work, most of it more on the middle management side of things than the changing children's lives side of things. An important trait in all of the most successful managers I've met is that they maintain a connection to what brought them to the field in the first place, so as not to get bogged down in the weight of the bureaucracy. For me, that means making sure no matter how complicated my responsibilities get, I make the time to teach regularly. It keeps me grounded in why I'm doing the rest of it in the first place, and keeps my skills sharp. It also prevents me from getting so divorced from the realities of the work that I start writing bad lessons. The classic win-win-win scenario.

Once you've made it to a full-time position in an institution, the trajectory and titles vary widely, but the overall trend is to become increasingly responsible for keeping the whole ship afloat. In my years full-time I've gone from being a manager, to a senior manager, to an associate director. In my current role I report directly to the VP for education, and oversee everything that relates to children in groups, both at the museum and out in the world. I have four full-time direct reports who oversee about sixty part-time direct reports, and I get to shape the way American history is taught for our entire institution. Not too shabby, for someone who once swore off history forever.

Part VI

The most pleasant surprise in all of this is that in my own, backward way, I've managed to become the academic scholar I always hoped I would become. For example, when I became an associate director, I took on the responsibility of attending curatorial meetings for upcoming exhibitions. This means I get to play a role in determining which stories are told at the New-York Historical Society, and help determine how those stories are told. When I attended my first meetings in this capacity I was terrified to speak up. I thought having only a master's degree, in a field far removed from American history, precluded me from having anything of value to add at a table full of tenured scholars and seasoned curatorial professionals. And there have been some capital-H Historians who have been startlingly dismissive. But in retrospect I think they would have been that way no matter how many letters came after my name. The vast majority have welcomed me and have given me space to share my thoughts and challenge their ideas. My eleven years in museum education gave me ample opportunities to research and think about history, and I've worked closely with the general public in a way that many academics never experience. I can speak with confidence about both the current state of historical thinking on a topic, and what the general public knows about it. Some scholars have even welcomed my ability to take ideas that haven't yet escaped the ivory tower, and broadcast them to a huge audience of hungry minds.

I'm also doing the original research and writing that are a hallmark of academia. I am part of a team creating a survey of American women's history for middle and high school students. I dive into dusty manuscript collections and find hidden gems that help illustrate women's experiences, and I'm doing the reading and writing to support it. The resulting online database, Women & the American Story, is the culmination of everything I have been working toward since I first decided to pursue graduate school. I cannot believe I've been lucky enough to land exactly where I wanted to be all those years ago.

In short, museum education has afforded me the opportunity, every day, to flex the interests and skills that brought me to academia in the first place. Whether it is reading a whole suite of books to cram for an upcoming exhibition, debating the interpretation of a source with people who are as interested as I am, or discovering new information in the archives that I can share with others to enrich our understanding of the past, museum education has given me the chance to do exactly what I dreamed of back as a naive undergraduate.

It wasn't until the editors of this book reached out to me about writing this essay that I realized there was an official name for what I've become, but I am glad to know now that I am an independent scholar. In my experience, the opportunities outside of academia are only expanding, and I'm glad that the growing use of this term means that people like me, who don't know what to do when they realize traditional academia isn't for them, might have an easier time finding their way to a career that is fulfilling and rewarding. So if you, dear reader, are someone who is struggling with the realization that traditional academia is not for you, know this: there is so much to do beyond the college campus, and we're waiting for you with open arms.

4

From the Ivory Tower to the Playground

DAYANNA KNIGHT

As a community college alumna who went on to an international doctoral program, I am well acquainted with the concept of academia being an "ivory tower," a place isolated from the realities of the outside world. Once upon a time, for a long time, I even dreamed that I would end up in some tenured niche within it, perhaps at a university with ivy-covered exteriors as old as the early medieval world that I study. In this dream my summers were filled with work on an excavation and my semesters punctuated by visits to museums and libraries packed with titles relevant to my research. These days I create coloring books. Medieval-themed coloring books.

Yes, you read that correctly. I am also the beloved on-site art instructor/archaeologist at a primary school in the Central Valley of California. Making that transition was not easy and, in some ways, it is ongoing. However, my journey so far has resulted in a significant shift in how I view academia. Before diving into my current thoughts though, I will provide (as we say in archaeology) a postmodernist reflection and the stratigraphy of my professional career. That is to say, I will give you my background before proceeding to the present day. I hope that sharing my story will help you, dear reader, on your own path.

Context

I began commonly enough. My mother fostered an interest in art in me from early on, providing quality supplies and opportunities, while my public school education was supplemented with hefty amounts of watching Public Broadcasting's finest and visiting my local libraries. When I wasn't in school, I also helped in my father's mechanic shop, which allowed me to acquire a rather interestingly diverse skill set. I discovered my interest in medieval studies by reading Tolkien in elementary school, found Vikings because of my seventh-grade teacher, and ultimately went into archaeological anthropology because of my need to figure out the why and how of people.

After high school I attended my local community college because, being a first-generation college student, I didn't want to ask my parents for money for university. I focused on people and their actions, chose my courses accordingly, and became incredibly lucky to have professors who genuinely loved teaching. By doing so I concurrently earned three Associate of Arts degrees: humanities, social sciences, and the last in liberal arts. I took courses in architectural drawing and rendering as well as civil ground surveying before I transferred in 2002 during my junior year to the anthropology department at the University of California, Berkeley. To help with the cost of my new school, I tutored in the Student Learning Center, sold concessions at the stadium, and even cleaned houses. I managed to earn enough from scholarships and working multiple jobs to finish my bachelor's degree in 2004 with only a few stints during which my husband and I ate spaghetti for a month straight. During my time at UC Berkeley I continued to make the most of my educational opportunities, doing things like drawing all my specimens from my osteology and human anatomy classes to use for studying. Looking back, some part of the neophyte medievalist I was then must have impressed my professor, because while I was still an undergraduate, I talked my way into the graduate-level Old Norse seminars. Maybe I truly was as convincing as I'd like to believe, or maybe I was really allowed to make that leap because my academically stellar professor recognized the benefits of an undergraduate in anthropology simultaneously learning the language of the medieval people she wanted to study. To this day I don't truly know why I was given permission, but am eternally grateful for it.

After graduation, it became clear that my continued interest in studying medieval archaeology was something universities in my home state on the West Coast of the United States were unable to properly accommodate, so I spent a couple of years hunting and applying for graduate programs that would help my career move closer to the North Atlantic archaeological sites that held my interest. Eventually I chose, for better and for worse, to attend graduate school at the University of Nottingham in the United Kingdom.

Initially my experience there was wonderful. As I worked on my master's degree, I was able to focus exclusively on the early medieval world. I even used my art background and took a class in archaeological graphics and publication in which I got to document eleventh-century Anglo-Scandinavian hogback sculptures. In an interesting twist, I was the only person that year who decided to take the course, so outside of my instructor and advisor, no one else in the department knew of my interest in art. It was like my little secret superpower.

In 2007, I transitioned into Nottingham's doctoral program,

where my first years were as full of ideas and networking as I'd pictured in my head. Graduate school very rarely goes exactly the way one intends, however. For some that can be beneficial. For others, the negative effects of the bumps in the road can increase their likelihood of dropping out of graduate school or can last long past graduation with their degree. I was one of the latter types of graduate students, and my experiences contributed to my path toward coloring book creation.

The third year of my doctoral program, 2010, became effectively derailed when the British Home Office began a cycle of visa denials. At a time when I should have begun sending in journal articles and teaching at the graduate level, I was instead preparing for immigration tribunals. It is no wonder that during this time I often dreamed of falling, always falling into the dark. Everyone, including me, believed I'd be flying back to California with little but the student loans on my back. I won the case, setting a legal precedent in the United Kingdom, but ultimately still had to return to California, which cost me a large part of the professional community I'd established at my university. Once home, I submitted my thesis internationally through Fed-Ex, then defended remotely via video conference in October 2013. I followed the graduation ceremony I should have walked in online and received my doctoral degree in the mail.

Although I began applying for university-level work before I defended, my lack of graduate-level teaching experience worked against me in the American university system so I took on a series of odd jobs including private tutoring and eventually began to substitute teach in primary education in fall 2015.

Professionally as an early career researcher and medievalist I was already watching the research world go by. I'd trained hard under some of the best in my field, at top schools, for the opportunity to run academic races but after all that happened during graduate school, I never made it out of the pasture, let alone competed on the track as an equal mind. My few hours of graduate teaching in the UK system in no way translated to the American job market beyond the single semester of community college adjuncting I secured in the final months before my verbal defense. That grated, but did not stop me. I had succeeded before when everyone (sometimes even myself) thought my situation was hopeless, and I was determined to do it again.

Early Work

In early 2015 I decided I needed to quit watching others run while waiting for my applications to be answered. If the British government couldn't stop my research, I owed it to myself and to the mentors who had believed in me to see if I could change the game. I made a simple chart for myself. The first column said, "What do departments do?" There I listed all the opportunities that the departments I had been in previously had supplied me. They ranged from library access to teaching opportunities, from intellectual camaraderie to project involvement. If your path, reader, is in any way like mine, this column will probably hurt to fill in. Think of it as pulling off a Band-Aid—do it and don't linger. The second column was "Can I do that myself?" Here I put "yes" or "no" depending on whether the item I listed in the first column was one I knew I could carry out independently. Filling in this column will probably feel better than the first. The final column was "How?" If I answered "yes" to something in the second column, I explained a method. If I answered "maybe," I put a potential idea. If I answered "no," I moved on until they were all done. Doing this allowed me to look at my skills in relation to my current situation and identify room for growth. I still refer to this list and work on it one item at a time.

Next, I started considering all of the options available to a specialist in the medieval Atlantic that could be acted upon from my inconvenient location in California. I could still produce quality illustration work from provided photographs. My work is better when I work on-site, or at least take the photos myself, but my situation is what it is. I drew up a few scenes. Then I took those scenes with me to the International Congress on Medieval Studies held in Kalamazoo, Michigan, in 2015. I showed those scenes to my friends and former colleagues in attendance. They were impressed and a little surprised to finally discover the illustration background I never had the chance to share amid the fight to keep me and mine from being deported back to the United States.

After Kalamazoo I assessed local public interest in the early medieval world of the Vikings by conducting library lectures and an activity day. Lecture audiences featured several demographics: older children and their parents, reenactors, and retired people of all ages. Each group had their own specific questions, but all of them believed the early medieval past consisted entirely of the aggressive burly male Viking stereotype. None of them knew about the rest of the woven tapestry of identity development based in family economics that my studies had allowed me to deeply explore. Some even used the poetry I read as medieval expressions of ethnography to justify abhorrent white supremacist attitudes. This situation, where a gap in public knowledge allowed stereotypes to foster violent expressions that could directly harm living populations, was one I sought to carefully rectify. People must have enjoyed them, because my events were popular and I ran out of both available chairs and activity supplies.

That same year, I was hired as a kindergarten through grade twelve substitute instructor and began teaching in the fall term. When my classes were good, I allowed time for them to color historical scenes I drew and ask questions. Guess which substitute teacher (whose writing you are reading right now) won Substitute of the Year in 2016-2017 in part for those efforts? I am proud that I established myself as the person everyone could count on to be both good at the job and able to genuinely get kids excited about learning and higher education. For instance, even though it's not necessary, I use my educational qualification at school so kids are exposed to the fact that female doctors exist, as do doctors in the humanities. It teaches them that maybe one day they can go on too. Back in the distant past when I was still working for the Student Learning Center at UC Berkeley there was a concept we regularly returned to during our meetings: as you climbed your mountain of success you had a duty to hold your hand back to help others up, too. I do my best to keep that philosophy in action.

By November 2015 I knew I wanted to focus on making a medieval coloring book that would help move the public past the violent stereotypes highlighted during the question and answer sessions of my library talks. However, I couldn't afford to stop substitute teaching due to my powerful attachment to eating, so I started looking into crowdfunding platforms. I figured that if many people could give just a little bit, I might be able to take some time off from teaching to get enough of a manuscript with illustrations together that a publisher would listen to me. Ideally, I wanted to produce this project through an academic publishing house so I could use their credibility to bolster my credentials as an independent scholar. By December I decided upon Kickstarter as my fundraising platform and figured out my social media strategy.

The Campaign Goes Live

I sat for several weeks on the official campaign before I went live with it. Putting something like this out into the world is a scary thing for an introvert. I hit "launch" and went to school to teach in January 2016, after winter break. That whole day I ignored my laptop until just before I went to bed—and I discovered I was already 20 percent toward my goal! I'd climbed onto the trapeze, built up speed, and jumped. Would I reach the next swing? That night I dreamed of falling, just as I used to when I was in the middle of my fight with the British Home Office. I woke up to being more than one-third of the way toward the goal. I set my posts for the day and went to work. On the third day I reached my goal. I emailed my local TV station, called my mom, tweeted to medievalists.net, and told the kids at my schools. All month we watched the level rise until it was just over double the original goal.

On the last day of the campaign, I was attending a conference held by my eventual publisher. I had emailed and arranged to meet one of the organizers at the event for some advice (someone I had discussed the idea of a coloring book with at the conference in Michigan). I brought my little portfolio of the few full scenes I had already completed and then mustered all my courage and asked a senior scholar which of the academic publishing houses he thought might be willing to try an outlandish idea like a medieval coloring book created by an independent scholar. It was an enjoyable conversation as he's someone who takes the role of mentoring younger researchers, even the ones who are not his to worry about, very seriously. If all established academics behaved this way, other independent scholars such as I would not feel quite so excluded from the rest of our respective fields. I knew my idea to address the public stereotype of aggressive Vikings and their heroic past through educational coloring books was good enough to take to a trade publishing house if I was not able to convince an academic publisher, but I still hoped that I could persuade one of them to take on my project.

The money from the campaign enabled me to purchase equipment, as well as take time off to do research. It's just like any other research grant in that respect. My young students beta tested most of the full scenes and are enormously proud of that now, although at the time they did not realize that I was going to do anything with my drawings. I didn't want to get their hopes up in case I failed in making an informative book. I decided to begin the Viking Coloring Book Project formally so I could be more official in my outreach efforts. *The Viking Coloring Book* was ultimately released by the Arizona Center for Medieval and Renaissance Studies Press (an academic publisher, just like I wanted!) in 2017, on the first day of school for my district. That was a brilliant feeling, but I knew that the real marketing work began now. I also plan to build on this project. I am currently working on the next title in the series: a coloring book inspired by Norse mythology.

Logistics

I want to take a step back and focus on the organization of all of this, for those who are interested in building their own campaign. Social media can be a dual-edged sword. Each platform functions as its own marketing network, which is often free to start on; but to create a robust marketing network is a serious investment of time at some level, whether it be for content creation or network maintenance.

Before I decided to run the Kickstarter campaign, I invested some of my time into using the basic methods of anthropological fieldwork I'd learned during my bachelor's. I began researching relative interest in certain hashtagged terms relevant to my work. This focused on those that were paid promotions begun by television shows. Doing this allowed me to figure out what would drive the market network I wanted to develop. Then I created marketing content catering to the trends and was able to gain initial interest quickly. The other part of my research time was spent figuring out a system of posting that kept high quality and consistent content across all platforms. I resolved this potentially overwhelming situation by posting to sites that I could then repost from to social media. My primary locations for posting before and during the campaign were my blog on Wordpress, *Viking Specialist at Large*, and my Instagram account, @vikingcoloringbookproject. I did extraordinarily little market grooming before launch, keeping my content to ongoing production photos combined with occasional descriptive written posts. My method has changed a little since I ran my first campaign as I now use a scheduling website to handle all my marketing posts. I still do commentary as well as random photos of behind the scenes, but moving to a scheduling system has freed up a lot of the time that I can now use for content creation.

Reflections

In many ways, although I certainly received a series of brutal knocks, I'm quite lucky that I am still standing and able to speak up. I'm female, but come from a lower working-class background that is white. If you've ever read Steinbeck's *The Grapes of Wrath* you will recognize the type. Being an independent scholar who is publicly vocal doing what I do would doubtlessly be much harder if I were not. My social media outreach, thankfully as of writing this, has not been a target of truly negative press. It could be quite different. There is currently an unfortunate, dark trend in the world of misunderstood and warped Viking history being commandeered for use by those with alt-right racist agendas. I am fortunate that people have looked at my work, which attempts to undo the horrific twisting of early medieval history, and have seen it for what it is, instead of assuming that my skin tone and chosen time period associate me with the wrong causes. It is my hope that through continuing my efforts, I will undermine those spreading falsehoods and bolster those with a genuine interest in a nuanced time period that is much more than has been portrayed by Hollywood and the press. In my published works I take away violent stereotypes and focus on the parts of the past that interacted with the wide beautiful and multicultural world. The parts that movies like to hide, behind a shield wall manned with faceless helmets.

As an independent scholar, when conducting my analysis and research for scene creation I try to follow along with global medieval research as it unfolds to the best of my abilities and internet access. I promote those who are in similar boats to mine. I pay attention to social media postings from early career researchers, academics of color, and first-generation scholars entering the tower system. When they say they are hurting, I try to help lessen their suffering through what means I have. This can take various forms, from sending funny photographs of my guinea pigs to reminding whoever it is that they aren't alone or helping arrange shared accommodations at a conference priced for those on tenure track—and sometimes it's by keeping my cyber-mouth shut and standing in silent support.

Currently my day job allows me the opportunity to influence the next generation of artists and researchers with the knowledge I learn from stories that are not my own. My reputation as a reliable substitute instructor recently resulted in my becoming an established art instructor at a primary school campus. I'm building the program from the ground up for all classes on-site. We paint and color, but we also take virtual field trips to online art galleries, internationally known exhibitions, and archaeological excavations. They learn that it's okay to make art just to make art, to have fun for one's own sake. They learn how art can build up communities as well as tear them down. But they also learn the power art can have to start conversations we are too frightened to have and provide a place to begin addressing changes in both heart and mind.

I know now that there is an incredibly good chance I'll only get to teach adults through my coloring books and other illustration works. Some days I regret that immensely as it feels as though I never got the chance to truly see what I was capable of academically once I'd gotten all the bureaucratic obstacles out of the way. Other days I have seminars with my young students, and they delve into the topics at hand just as readily, sometimes more so than adults, and with less of the established biases. I have *fun* at my job daily. Genuine laugh-out-loud fun every day. After the traumatic experiences of graduate school, that is a lot more important than it might have otherwise been. Although I do grade hundreds of papers, they are visual instead of written, so I'm not stuck slogging through three hundred undergraduate conceptions of the same topic in essay form multiple times a term. I really do engage with hundreds of young students, because I teach every grade level at some point during any given week. The kids like to put notes to me in among their portfolio work about how much they like art, me, the topic, or even one time how they'd like to have butlers for an event that was planned. They also put in the drawings they make outside of school that are inspired by topics we discussed in class. We talk about what they want to see next or learn how to do or even what art they saw on their real field trips to other places. I show them I care about them as well as the topics, so they care about themselves in addition to what is in the curriculum. In many ways I feel like I do decent work where I get to use my practical skills. My students still love learning as they have not yet had experiences that could leave them jaded. That is no small feat, given what people, even children, especially children, have access to that competes to capture their interest in the world today.

Is all that early groundwork vital for someone to matriculate into higher education? Absolutely. Is it recognized as the necessary foundation for much greater things in students of any age? In my experience, not nearly enough. Often, people with the same university-level training that I completed ignore the fact the groundwork even exists, and I find that incredibly hurtful. Again here I have been lucky and only had to have direct conversations about those views a few times, most often during interviews. The first occurred after the interviewer listened to my full background and then said, "But do you have any more graduate-level teaching experience?" The second occurred during an interview for a nonacademic role performed by academics during events at several institutions. There, it was more blatant: "We have Nobel laureates in attendance at these events. As you work with children, we don't think you are capable of speaking to our guests without embarrassing them." I responded with a polite version of, "Well then my doctoral program should not have awarded me my doctoral degree, but they did, so someone more qualified in my field than you seemed to realize that I can talk to whomever wants to learn" and then hung up. As you can imagine, I try not to put myself in those situations much these days as they are unnecessarily vexing. Making the decision to do so allows me more freedom to use my true voice and bring up issues I might not dare to raise if I was attached to an institution. As I reminded a senior academic during an unwanted email exchange, I have no qualms about telling someone at a university they are being rude as I no longer exist in that system. I have no hope of employment there no matter how hard I try, so why would I waste my time coddling academic egos expressing nothing but social superiority over me? The kindergarteners I teach have more sense than that.

Medieval Studies as an Independent Scholar

I wish I could tell you it's been easy to negotiate a humanities research field like medieval studies as an independent scholar. In my case it's not been smooth, although I suspect if I were closer to the networks I'd developed in graduate school I might feel differently. Now I am effectively on the night shift in comparison to those networks as I'm several time zones away. Being out of sight and effectively out of the mind of everyone makes it quite difficult to get involved in even the projects constructed in such a way that I could be included if I lived closer. However, when I do have an innovative idea that I am able to act upon from start to finish, the early medieval network I still have has been incredibly good about coming together in support.

In many ways I worry about wearing out my welcome in that network. Very few adult people engage with what I do directly through contact with me, whether at conferences or online. More do so through my coloring books, when I am not present. That is another regret, I suppose. My young students are awesome, but they can't replace the invaluable discussion that comes from being in a research group of peers. It is often painful to lack that aspect. I've tried addressing it by forcing myself to be more involved in societies, but I find myself repeatedly staring at long lists of boards and committees being filled by only established traditional academics. No one speaks for me, no one watches for my kind in these groups where membership fees are exorbitant and often equal to the fees independent scholars must pay to access academic journals. Sadly, jumping this financial hurdle and becoming a member is often the only way to be eligible for the few grants that are inclusive of independent scholars. To participate in academic medievalist initiatives for kindergarten through grade twelve outreach I am expected to donate my hard work to a system that only selectively sees me, yet it never seems to occur to these institutions that including membership as part of the prize would increase their outreach as a result. It is disappointing that they would prefer to force truly independent scholars to decide between memberships and journal access instead of creating more inclusive requirements.

When I meet new academics, often my outreach efforts are talked down to, as though I did not earn a doctorate in the field. Rather annoyingly, the experience keeps repeating. From grants that allow the funding of research to speaking opportunities to the chances to review books, all of these opportunities are effectively out of reach for many medievalists who are also independent scholars. Once, when trying to get involved with conference organization I was informed that I'd be allowed to service the coffee table on the day of the event.

I suspect I am not the only person feeling such frustration at the constantly closed doors, so I try to remind academics of their privileges with regard to things like libraries, attending conferences, and the organization of those conferences when they post on social media. It's not done to single them out or force them to feel institutional guilt, but rather for the other people reading posts that feel like me: those scholars on the outside, the ones that only get to read articles if someone goes open access or posts it on academia .edu. We can often feel as though we get only the crumbs from the bounty of knowledge's table where we once had a place to sit. I can and do articulate ideas for improvement and hope someone reads, understands, and eventually acts upon them to make the situation better. Until then, others that read my comments might feel better knowing that they are not alone and who knows, maybe someday those other independent medievalists will feel up to contacting me, ready to do more. I can always use more friends.

What's Next?

Aside from lesson planning at school, I am working on the next titles in my early medieval coloring book series. Instead of Kickstarter, this time I am funding through sales of art, toys, and games that allow people of all ages to safely explore the early medieval world.

I create materials that exploit the moment of interest to expose the public to more in-depth knowledge about the medieval past. The Norse mythology–themed Viking coloring book is about half done as I write this. After that I will begin the first stages of a female-themed volume as well as one on travel. Classes have already started to give me feedback about the scenes I've shown them, and since the children now have a better idea of what I'm attempting, it helps them focus a bit more. We have a lot of conversations about all sorts of topics because of this approach, from medieval gender to animals that people in the past would have recognized to questions about my process and methods of production.

I tell the kids about what it's like to go to conferences in the humanities, to see friends that only make it together at roundtable panels. My students want to experience what that's like so I am working on making that happen in such a way that they have the agency to create but are safe. My first steps toward a virtual humanities conference where kids, academics, and those professionals like me who are working somewhere in between can interact and exchange ideas have gone well, and I am hopeful for the future.

I have also become more outspoken about what I do. I remind people that I'm available for commissioned works of all types, from full scenes, architectural renderings of private homes and pet portraits, to maps and more traditional archaeological illustration. Sometimes it works, sometimes not, but since it's not the only role paying my bills it's something I act on only when the opportunity arises. I sell my art directly and through the books I create in order to spark the questions that I hope I would have received if I was teaching in a university. I am frank about the fact that I'd not get to use the knowledge I fought a government for the right to finish if I'd not begun to make coloring books. *The Viking Coloring Book* has opened doors for me, leading to opportunities such as what you are reading now. In a small way it's starting to get me access to the writing and publication opportunities that I was denied while fighting the aforementioned government. Considering that, maybe eventually I'll get to publish something properly academic.

Maybe eventually I won't have the weight of imposter syndrome on my shoulders, whispering the cruelest of ideas about my self-worth in my ears. When I can ignore those plaguing thoughts and focus on the bigger picture, I see that I make coloring books about what I love to research so that the next generation will save my field from disappearing, and I know that I am already successful. I've experienced firsthand what kind of interest my work inspires. I've created my own place to play, and it's a much better place to be than one where I let my lack of a role in the ivory tower world keep me down.

5

Footnoting History *for the Public*

CHRISTINE CACCIPUOTI
and
ELIZABETH KEOHANE-BURBRIDGE

Growing up, we were drawn to the idea that the best path for those who excelled at school was to become a scholar, without a possible qualifying term identifying anyone as "independent." We looked up to illustrious academics and wanted to be like them, researching our favorite historical periods and getting paid to do it, while also imparting that knowledge to others through teaching and publishing. It would have been extraordinarily precocious of us to entertain the idea of fulfilling these goals with podcasting because in the late eighties and early nineties when we fantasized about adulthood, podcasting did not exist. Yet here we are, independent scholars producing a successful podcast called *Footnoting History* that reaches thousands of people from the United States and Singapore to Kenya and Ireland every single day. Did our lives go exactly to plan? No. Do we love what we do? Yes.

Once Upon a Dream

While in graduate school at Fordham University, where we met as classmates in 2007, the concept of an "independent" scholar (meaning one who still participates in academic activities without an official affiliation with a college or university) was still not truly on our radars. This period was consumed by so much work that completing our degrees was the focus, not what we would be called by others after we earned them. It is perhaps not surprising that we became friends. On paper our backgrounds are very similar (we both are white women who grew up in New York, attended Catholic schools, love pop culture, and get very, very excited about history), and Fordham fostered student friendship simply because we often had multiple classes with the same people, our fellow burgeoning medievalists. Now, over a decade after those halcyon days of stressing about papers and discussing life together at various Italian restaurants on the Bronx's Arthur Avenue, our continued contact with our larger group of friends is enabled by social media platforms like Facebook. As for us personally, we evolved from classmates to coworkers to a level we regularly describe as "female Cory and Shawn" from *Boy Meets World*, the 1993–2000 sitcom that followed the coming-of-age experiences of the aforementioned best friends—one of whom, it should be noted, grew up to become, in the next incarnation of the show, a history teacher (we will let those of you familiar with the show decide which of us is Cory and which is Shawn). (Elizabeth yells, "They want you to take the rolls!" at this suggestion.)

There was a sense of security within Fordham's walls. As stressful as the work could be (and who among us did not, at least once, wonder if we were truly "good enough" to finish—impostor syndrome, friends, is very real) our network helped us get through. If this sounds nostalgic that's because it is. Our time in graduate school was a strange experience where we were not yet full adults in the occupational sense but were also certainly no longer the children we had been when we first stepped onto our respective undergraduate campuses. For many (including ourselves) graduate school is the last time you have before being kicked out of the figurative nest into the unknown of the real world. Embracing this social experience kept us sane and gave us fond memories.

Ultimately we only overlapped at Fordham for a year and a half. In May 2008, Christine received her MA and opted not to pursue her doctorate. She bowed out of traditional academia without ever applying to a PhD program, something that surprised even herself. There were multiple factors involved in this decision, including burnout. By the time she completed graduate school, she had applied to colleges three times in six years: as a high school senior, when she decided to transfer out of her original undergraduate college, and after graduating from Fordham College Lincoln Center with her BA. Her final semester of graduate school was particularly trying because it included writing a thesis on canonical bigamy in the medieval English church, an incredibly niche topic that, while certainly unique, was so far removed from her interests in twelfth-century English royalty that it was more of a chore than a satisfying experience of scholarly engagement. (If you are wondering why she did not choose her thesis topic based on her interests, the answer was a matter of timing: by entering the program in the spring term she missed the chance to join a seminar on medieval England and therefore fell into the next one, centered on church law. While it was a class she certainly had interest in, it was not something she wanted to spend any period of time working on as the defining product of her degree.)

Writing the bigamy thesis did a great deal to increase her abilities as a historian, but it also involved constant reminders from her advisor that academic writing should never have personality.

Her writing, he informed her, was very good but needed to be drier for academia to embrace it. It physically pained her to remove her voice from her writing, and she reconsidered whether she had a desire to write for an academic audience if it always required this sort of censorship.

In addition, she never forgot considerations raised by two beloved mentors years prior: that the dissertation process could be very isolating and depressing, and if she did not have classroom teaching as a goal (she certainly did not) then nonacademic hiring committees might view her as "too educated" or as someone who would leave as soon as a better, likely academic, job came along. Although she dreamed of being called "Dr. Caccipuoti," Christine determined the path it would lead her down was not one that she wanted to travel. Her interests were in researching, writing, and storytelling, but she lacked any drive to do that in a classroom. Obtaining her PhD was a goal because she wanted to prove she could do it and be viewed as an expert in her field, not because she had a desire to join the professoriate. The fact that teaching was viewed as the primary (or, really, only) acceptable occupation for a PhD was disheartening, and she could not bring herself to invest up to a decade of her life on a project that would largely qualify her only for a job she did not want, no matter how much she adored her field and graduate school in general or how hard it was to watch her friends continue their studies without her.

Meanwhile, Elizabeth had, since at least high school, considered becoming a history professor. There was a short detour after undergrad where she worked as a paralegal and a special education teacher mainly because the idea of applying to graduate school and partaking in a MA/PhD program that would take at least five years (Elizabeth laughs now at that thought of finishing in such a short time frame) left her anxious. Since graduating high school, Elizabeth hadn't spent more than two years in one place—she transferred after her freshman year, did her junior year abroad, and followed somewhat similar patterns in her jobs. Yet, here she was contemplating a process that would "lock her down" to one location for the remainder of her twenties. Ultimately, though, she applied to and chose Fordham for the MA. After a year there, all fears of being in one program with one cohort vanished, and Fordham was the only school to which she applied for the PhD. In these early hazy lovely years, she still very much wanted to become a tenured professor who wore tweed and popped up on C-SPAN's *Book Talk* so her father would get to see her on television. She loved her teaching and research dreams and even had mental outfits picked out for those future appearances.

Her work, though, did not occur in a vacuum. In her second year of the PhD program and first year with a teaching fellowship, Elizabeth got married. Then, during the dissertation-writing process, she gave birth to three children, moved from New York to Georgia, and taught as an adjunct. As she will tell anyone, her dissertation proposal was accepted a week before her eldest child's birth. The move physically removed her from our graduate school cohort, that vital support group. She had to make her way in a new location, struggle to schedule affordable child care to enable her writing, cope with sleep deprivation, and support her husband as he obtained his second MS while she was still writing about late medieval English church convocations. Elizabeth had avoided student loans, but this meant that child care was not an option. Adjuncting, which helped pay for child care, took up all the time her children were at day care or preschool, leaving her no time for writing. It was not ideal.

Elizabeth was always aware that people—including her advisor—likely believed she would not finish, based on all the developments in her life. She wanted to prove them wrong and pushed forward, but not without wishing she had more child care support at home and a greater number of champions in her corner. Although, initially, her sister and father had been able to help, they both lived out of state, and Elizabeth felt guilty for taking them away from their lives. In addition, she knew that she worked best in situations where her writing was regularly discussed with others or at least reviewed at short intervals. Without our cohort nearby, this was difficult to arrange, plus her advisor expected to review her writing only at the completion of each drafted chapter. The process was not optimized to foster her highest level of production, which contributed to some of her less-positive feelings about it all. However, the more she wrote the closer she got to obtaining that long-desired PhD, so she continued, with her writing and revising process based on the old adage: How do you eat an elephant? One bite at a time. (Note from Christine, the adorer of elephants: please never actually eat an elephant.)

As with Christine, Elizabeth's plans for the future changed once she took stock of her situation. She learned that universities in Georgia were shifting away from a structure that included tenure-track lectureships, which did not bode well for her. She had already started to become involved in her new local community and would have to go through the whole integration process again if she got a job requiring her family to relocate. Also, she was increasingly aware that during the academic hiring process many establishments placed a high level of importance on prior publications, and her CV only held one published journal article. As her defense neared, Elizabeth grappled with the understanding that while her future would always include tweed, she might never wear it as a tenured professor at a Georgia university.

Then, with a toddler and a four-month-old, no child care, a dissertation still in draft form, and adjuncting two classes at a time, she decided, as one does, to start a podcast.

A Whole New World

Like any other technological medium, podcasts developed over a long period of time. Most often though, podcasts in their current form are credited as the product of a collaboration between David Winer and Christopher Lydon in the early 2000s.[1] By 2004, journalist Ben Hammersley was pondering what to call this new recorded-audio phenomenon and suggested the term "podcast." (He also tossed out "audioblogging" and "GuerillaMedia," but we think the best suggestion won.)[2] It didn't take long before podcasts properly entered into popular consciousness. In October 2005, the popular teen drama *One Tree Hill* included a scene where Marvin "Mouth" McFadden (played by Lee Norris) asked his basketball-player friend Nathan Scott (played by James Lafferty) if he would mind giving an interview for his podcast. Nathan's response of "Podcasting?" is indicative of the bemused curiosity around the country that year. Mouth explained, "It's kind of like radio, but the fans can download it and listen to it on their iPods," but he was not alone in explaining this new concept.[3] Mere months later the *New Oxford American Dictionary* made "podcast" its Word of the Year, and provided a formal definition: "A digital audio file made available on the internet for downloading to a computer or mobile device, typically available as a series, new installments of which can be received by subscribers automatically."[4]

When Elizabeth had her spark of creativity in 2013, podcasting was still something of a wild frontier. Podcasts could (and still can) be started by anyone, anywhere, with any agenda. Some of the earliest history podcasts were popular but were rarely spearheaded by actual historians. Elizabeth was listening to one such show when her mind wandered to the notion of working for them. A quick Google search brought her to the hiring page for the show: they wanted freelancers to submit scripts that the hosts might or might not record at some point. No, Elizabeth thought, if she was going to do the research and write and prepare a script, she would be the one hosting the show.

On January 9, 2013, Elizabeth sent a Facebook message to a group of her historian friends (including Christine) proposing her idea. The as-yet-unnamed podcast would feature the same exciting anecdotes that we loved to share with each other but that rarely made it into the body of our scholarly texts and would be approximately ten to twenty minutes per episode. The show length was deliberate: Elizabeth found it hard to complete an entire episode of popular history podcasts (many were over an hour long!) and was never quite sure when she would be able to return to them. A show of a shorter length would give a person an opportunity to escape into the past while commuting or cooking dinner or fitting a moment of respite into a child's naptime. Our easily digestible podcast, perfect for the busy listener, would teach the public riveting things from history and dispel the negative stereotype of the stuffy, unapproachable academic historian locked away in an ivory tower of elitism. Naturally, the majority of the group was immediately all in.

This was the first time Christine grappled with being a so-called independent scholar. She was five years removed from graduate school and her goals no longer included anything traditionally academic. She sought to write factually sound, realistic historical fiction and popular nonfiction and to advance long-standing performing objectives. By 2013, she had worked her way into the acting union SAG-AFTRA and would soon also join Actors' Equity, thus realizing a dream she had harbored since seeing her first Broadway show (Disney's *Beauty and the Beast*) in 1995. She was working to build a publication résumé (her first short story would be published in 2015), and wondered whether her time away from academia diminished her legitimacy as a qualified historian worthy of participating in the podcast. People outside of academia never questioned her credentials, but she was unsure of the reception from insiders—including some of her friends. Could you still be called a historian without a PhD? What about without working in a university, or teaching in any capacity? Her self-doubt lingered but was never allowed to prevail because there was no time to wallow with our launch date looming.

We do not suggest trying to launch a podcast in a month with stars in your eyes and no experience under your belt. It was a whirlwind period of decisions, largely made by committee. We needed a name (*Footnoting History!*), hosting platform and website, social media channels, a release schedule, and of course, to create episodes. A natural administration team emerged quickly with Elizabeth as producer, Christine as assistant producer, and Nathan Melson as audio editor, while our nine other participating friends contributed episodes and completed our rotation.

On February 2, 2013, we released our first episode, "Lambert Simnel and Perkin Warbeck: Pretenders to the Throne?" recorded by Elizabeth. We eagerly watched as tens (yes, that many!) of people discovered us and hoped they were not just our family. When we received positive reviews, we celebrated. We shared our episodes on our personal social media channels, registered with different podcast apps, and cultivated a following through our podcast's Facebook and Twitter accounts, but mostly we kept creating content and putting it out into the world to draw an audience through our (hopefully) enticing topics. *Footnoting History* required daily attention if we wanted to make something of it.

Just Around the Riverbend

The years between launching *Footnoting History* and Elizabeth becoming an independent scholar were filled with lessons and development. We graduated from recording using free apps on our phones and sitting under blanket forts (literally, we have the pictures to prove it—the blanket forts minimized echoes) to purchasing actual microphones. It became apparent that a dozen hosts were simply too many (both to wrangle and to expect our subscribers to remember well enough to build listener–podcaster relationships) and that weekly episodes were too much, so we tweaked the formula, slowly shrinking our rotation from twelve hosts to six and shifted from releasing episodes every week to every other week. We discovered the importance of defining historical vocabulary and treating each episode as a monologue—one that was dynamic and showcased our enthusiasm. We learned that we tended to talk too fast and had to train our brains to create short, snappy titles instead of long, cumbersome ones better suited for specialist conferences than public consumption.

We knew enough to ask for help, and were incredibly lucky that a friend Elizabeth made in a mom group was in broadcasting. Elizabeth's friend, Christy Fajardo, journalist for KCBS-TV in Los Angeles, and her cousin who worked for NPR, listened to an episode from each contributor and provided excellent feedback and helpful hints, such as, "Smile when you are stating a happy event—it will be conveyed in your tone." As we made these adjustments, positive responses started to come in from people other than our family and friends.

Our most notable piece of press from the early years came in October 2015, when the Canadian Broadcasting Corporation's Podcast Playlist included us on their list, "Ten History Podcasts You Need to Hear," alongside famous shows like Dan Carlin's *Hardcore History* and *Stuff You Missed in History Class*.[5] The article included a suggested episode for each podcast, and for us it was Christine's "The Royal Teeth of Louis XIV," which covered the difficulties endured by France's Sun King as his teeth rotted and required removal. That episode sprang to the top of our most-downloaded list (it was eventually our first episode to reach twenty-one thousand downloads) and did wonders for Christine's impostor syndrome, sparking the epiphany that not only was she capable of being a public historian but she was also quite good at it.

As Christine was finally accepting her competency as a scholar, Elizabeth was juggling podcasting with preparing to both defend her dissertation and leave traditional academia. In spring 2016 she accepted a position teaching high school history at Woodward Academy in the Atlanta metro area, and the job's start date was the same week as her defense. As Elizabeth would find, beginning this job meant that any future traditional scholars she met would know her primarily as a high school teacher and would quite possibly view her as below them, or as a failure.

In academia there is an unofficial hierarchy, with a structure reminiscent of a target, where the bull's-eye consists of established academic scholars who are either tenured or tenure-tracked. Outside that core is a ring holding graduate students and all adjuncts or nontenured lecturers and professors, basically those still within the college or university fold. By taking this job, Elizabeth was transitioning from the second to the third ring, that of the independent scholar with graduate training who works in an educational field outside of a college or university (this ring also includes those who work at museums, libraries, historical sites, etc.). She was, for many graduate students, seen as a sort of cautionary tale, although it was hard to point out what she did "wrong" exactly, and the fact that she never even bothered to apply to a tenure-track position seemed to leave many befuddled. While she was still closer to the core than Christine (her decidedly nonhistorical employment exiled her even farther out in Independent Scholar Land), the change from insider to outsider occurred almost immediately. Now we were both trying to cope with the challenge of working outside of academia while also dealing with the increasing production demands of *Footnoting History*.

Poor, Unfortunate Souls

No one can take away the education you received, but they can take away the tools you need to succeed in your field. After a brief grace period following her graduation back in 2008, Christine lost remote access to her alma mater's library resources—a standard procedure in many American universities. Even if she paid the annual alumni fee for book-borrowing privileges, digital access would not be included. To say this elicited a moment of panic is an understatement, as it would be impossible to visit a Fordham campus every time she needed to conduct research. Luckily, her circle of friends rallied and shared resources the same way others traded Netflix passwords. As thankful for her friends as she was, she did not like this arrangement and would still happily pay to access the databases remotely if it was an option, but it is not. Eventually, Elizabeth too was cut off, although (demonstrating the aforementioned target structure of academia) she retained some access through Woodward Academy.

Our only choice was to investigate places we could access. We are thankful to institutions like the New York Public Library for their extensive subscriptions open to those who live anywhere in New York State and JSTOR, the academic journal database that provides a variety of free and paid subscription options for individual researchers. Historical societies, museums, and libraries are increasingly digitizing their holdings, and we collect links to those with relish. There are holdouts though, as some collections and databases specifically state that they will not offer subscriptions to individuals and are only interested in working with institutions. While some academic databases have astronomical pricing for individuals, at least the offer is there. To completely deny access to individuals is a loss for both the writers (whose work will not be widespread) and the outside scholars (who will not be able to read it).

Access issues can heavily influence one's level of production compared to traditional scholars. For *Footnoting History* we both write four episodes per year, and because we do not stick to a specific theme, these topics are often entirely new to us. Without ready access to university resources, sometimes exciting topics have to wait because we are not able to make the trek to campus to get the book we need or read the necessary articles in time for our next release date, so we opt for something we can do based on what we already have in our possession. Our topic selections, therefore, are dictated by both interest and accessibility, but that is not the only thing impacted by being an independent scholar.

Leaving academia also alters how you are perceived personally and professionally. We both encountered a distinct change in the way we were treated upon leaving Fordham. For Christine, leaving first and working entirely outside of the field, it was obvious that people assumed she was no longer a historian. They occasionally asked her to read things and comment on them, but more often than not she was excluded. Some might have even quietly believed she was no scholar at all, given her lack of continued overtly academic ties. It is regularly assumed that independent scholars might not be qualified to partake in serious historical discussions as if, by some bizarre act of magic, leaving academia removes all of their abilities. This, of course, is absurd.

After her defense, Elizabeth's experience was similar with people she already knew, but the exclusion was more pointed when it came to those she was meeting for the first time. At one well-known history conference for which she flew across the Atlantic to give a paper, she had the misfortune of encountering academics who, upon learning of her employment at a high school, commented on how quaint it was for her to attend the conference to indulge her hobby. This sort of interaction can be both deflating and enraging, because it can make you question your place and also proves that there are others determined to keep you out based on who provides your paycheck. People who deny the validity of your presence or talk down to you are going to exist, and we wish we could say that we have never let it bother us. Still, it hurts when your friends stop involving you, or show less interest in your projects than you do in theirs, and it also hurts when you meet new colleagues who care more about the affiliation on your name tag than your actual abilities. What is important is finding the good people, and keeping them close. We are lucky that we have each other and are always there to commiserate when a bad experience occurs—and then to follow it up with plans for world domination, because we won't let others determine the course of our lives.

Let It Go

Fortunately, *Footnoting History* more than makes up for the incidents that cause broken hearts and dips in confidence. It grew, slowly at first, and then picked up speed once we implemented our rotation adjustments. We cheered when our download numbers entered into the millions and our reach extended beyond just majority-English-speaking countries. What our listeners care about more than our place on the academic target model is that we accurately cover topics they enjoy. We use our platform to try to inspire our listeners to delve deeper into the topics we discuss by providing further reading suggestions, and we are always available through email or social media to answer questions. We began to make a name for ourselves and were invited to present at the Rocky Mountain Medieval and Renaissance Association in spring 2014, where Elizabeth and some of our contributors spoke to scholars who were interested in using this new form of media to reach those interested in history. By and large our interactions have been positive and our listeners enthusiastic about our product.

When it comes to running *Footnoting History*, we don't believe in differentiating among socially constructed types of scholars. We are open about who we are in our episodes, mentioning personal details pertinent to our topic selections, but no host is considered more important than another. From the onset we have had our credentials listed on *Footnoting History*'s website but, as of writing this, not one subscriber has ever questioned our status as scholars. If you were to listen to one episode from each host in a row, without knowing who we were, you would not be able to differentiate the independent from the traditional scholars based on our presentations. What matters is the content and how well the story is conveyed. Translating academic history into a form suitable for all ranges of the public is a skill we have worked hard to hone. It requires taking in large amounts of information and synthesizing it, then distilling it down to only what a person needs to know in order to get a grasp on the people or events being discussed. That makes it like teaching, but without the visual aspect. Our subscribers cannot see us, so we lack the ability to provide visual aids or even rely upon our facial expressions to convey our messages. Everything must come out through a careful combination of word selection and intonation, like a radio play. We must speak clearly and at a pace that does not cause the story to drag but that still allows our audience to absorb material that may possibly be entirely new to them. It is a delicate balance, one that is sometimes hard to judge when you record without an audience.

Every episode we do is entirely self-contained, which is different from a classroom setting where one piece often builds upon another. Many podcasts revolve wholly around one field of history (think ancient Greece or the US Civil War), but we are a general history podcast, which means at any given time our six hosts could be recording episodes set in six different countries and six different centuries. Although some people or events may be repeatedly mentioned, we cannot guarantee that our listeners today have heard past episodes, so we must include enough information to prevent a new listener from getting lost while ensuring that a regular subscriber won't get bored by repetition. Our product is free and the vast majority of our listeners are following us by choice. Their decision to trust us with their precious time means everything, and we do not want to disappoint, so we care very much about quality control and continued improvement.

Something else happened too, while we were trying to please the public. We learned that we were also pleasing academics. Admittedly, we had the moral support of Fordham's history department from the beginning. Although we are fully independent, knowing our former professors and mentors appreciate our endeavor has been a true source of encouragement. We are particularly thankful to Drs. Nicholas Paul and Maryanne Kowaleski for cheering us on, but they knew us when we still were active in traditional academia. They taught and advised us for years before *Footnoting History* launched, so they knew the extent of our abilities better than those first encountering us through our episodes. The support of academics who met us through the podcast took years to cultivate.

While nothing may change the mind of those that believe academia should remain a cloistered realm away from the public eye, others are growing increasingly curious about bringing history to the public and finding new ways to engage their students. Many of these internet-savvy academics are turning to podcasts like ours to enhance their lessons. Although we never choose a topic for the purpose of it being used in a classroom, we appeal to educators by addressing aspects of history that are not normally discussed. Through episodes like "American Indian Prisoners of War" and "Guy de Montfort and Dante's *Inferno*," we provide compact yet in-depth explanations of historical events that might not appear in the standard curriculum. These allow educators to diversify the information they provide their students. In addition to the traditional textbook, they can now bring in historians (us) to enhance their lessons with the push of a button. To make using our episodes easy for them, we feature a database specifically for educators on FootnotingHistory.com that sorts our episodes by geographic location, time period, and theme, and also provide some sample assignments created by Elizabeth.

In late 2016, Averill Earls of the then-upcoming history podcast *Dig* contacted us about joining her and her coproducer Marissa Rhodes on a panel to discuss podcast creation at the 2017 Berkshire Conference of Women Historians. We welcomed the opportunity to return to the belly of the academic beast and spoke to a group of open-minded, interested academics about how to build history podcasts that appeal to the public. For this event, our listed affiliation was *Footnoting History*, and no one questioned our right to be there. Instead (much to our surprise!) many people stopped us to comment positively on our work and express admiration at our expertise. It was one of the first times we met listeners in person, and that made it particularly special.

In 2018 we followed this experience by speaking at Sound Education, the first annual conference held at Harvard University for the express purpose of discussing education through the medium of podcasting. Academia has not only noticed podcasting, but they are embracing it to the point that it has its own conference on an Ivy League campus. Here all attendees used their podcast as their affiliation. We walked around with *Footnoting History* proudly displayed on our badges, mingling with all forms of educational podcasters, from the corporate sponsored to the independent, the academic to the popular, and everything in between. We recognized the names of people we listen to and were floored more than once when people approached us because of our apparent reputation. It may sound ridiculous, but most of our listeners are represented only by numbers, so we never expect any people we meet to be subscribers, even if they now number in the tens of thousands. It is entirely possible that the sensation of surprise that accompanies recognition will never get old.

The increasing acceptance of podcasting panels into conferences for traditional academics and the creation of events like Sound Education prove that podcasting is gaining recognition in the scholarly world. When it comes to embracing the influential abilities of podcasting, academia is following in the wake of pop culture, where podcasting is now a behemoth. Every celebrity out there seems to have a podcast, and some people who began as podcasters have turned into celebrities. In the decade-plus since Mouth explained podcasting to Nathan on *One Tree Hill*, television has evolved its inclusion of podcasts, too. Some podcasts like *Dirty John* and *2 Dope Queens* amassed such popularity that they earned pod-to-screen adaptations, while in 2018 CBS debuted a drama called *God Friended Me* in which the main character is, you guessed it, a podcaster. That academia is starting to embrace this medium that has already proven itself as a useful tool of mass communication is heartening.

As more and more universities create their own podcasts, debates have emerged about who has the "right" to podcast about history. To us, what defines a "legitimate" history podcaster is the quality of their work, and you don't need to have a PhD and teach at a top university to meet that criterion. In fact, some academics make downright awful podcasters, just as some podcasters would make awful traditional academics. The only people who decide a person's "right" to podcast are the subscribers. They give their blessing by increasingly listening to episodes, leaving positive ratings, and telling their friends to listen, too. We became well-known not because academia immediately adored us, but because our listeners did and academia could not ignore the growing trend. Although we love seeing podcasts gain ground with the traditionally employed crowd, and there is certainly ample room for university-produced podcasts alongside independent ones, we earned our place in the history podcasting world without a built-in institutional audience, which is a source of deep personal pride.

Go the Distance

Make no mistake, we did not transition from future academics to current podcasters easily or overnight, and we are still learning and growing. Podcasting is what we are known for, but we maintain the jobs we took immediately after graduate school. Sometimes this means answering emails between debate team events (Elizabeth) or writing a script while wearing a period costume (Christine), at other times it means traveling to a conference on your weekend off or recording when everyone else has gone to bed. The podcast is still largely self-funded although the group has discussed incorporating advertising. Most often, advertising adds time to episodes. Our target audience prefers their episodes on the short end, and an ad that would seem short in a lengthy podcast would feel enormous to our listeners, unless we could find the right partner. We relish our autonomy and are quite careful about our associations, because we never want to reach a place where a third-party financial investor dictates our content. At present our income comes from merchandise sales and Patreon—which allows fans to support us through monthly subscriptions in exchange for merchandise (and our eternal gratitude). While that has helped to offset production costs like website hosting fees, we have yet to reach a point where any individual podcaster can be paid. Overall though, while we would love to one day receive paychecks large enough for *Footnoting History* to be our primary occupation (or at least pay for a group holiday), we do it for free because we enjoy it and it enables our participation in academic conversations as independent scholars.

When we were in school, there were no classes about developing unique careers or even searching for history-related jobs outside of academia. Although most history departments have websites that list all the occupational options for undergraduate history majors, when you reach the graduate level it is typically assumed that a career within academia is the goal. Preparing MA and PhD students to use what they've learned outside of the university was not a priority in many departments during our educational period. Now, though, it seems that universities are realizing that the percentage of their students that will follow the traditional route is shrinking, and they are beginning to offer guidance and suggestions. We wish we had had that, because the truth is that we stumbled into podcasting somewhat by luck. If Elizabeth had not begun listening to history podcasts while doing data entry on clergy who died over six hundred years ago, or if none of our friends were receptive to the idea, or if we gave up due to the difficulty of finding time to wrangle our podcasters and market ourselves, we would not be here now. There is a term used for people like us, "alt-acs," which refers to people who work in alternative (read "nontraditional") academic careers, but we prefer to think of it as expanded academics. We are part of the group of scholars who work as academics in new and exciting ways to reach a broader audience, and that is vital to the continuation of our field.

The podcast landscape is littered with shows launched with the best of intentions that did not last beyond their first year, for reasons we may never know. This clutter can make it difficult for new shows to find footing, and podcasting can be like the race for the cornucopia in Suzanne Collins's novel *The Hunger Games.* Everyone starts off with zero listeners; as they rush toward their potential audience at full speed, they are hoping to reach them first and get more listeners than anyone else and are willing to knock others out of the way. Podcasting is likely not going to get less competitive until some other new medium is developed that takes over the space, but you do not need to be brutal. Content and consistency will eventually push you to the front of the pack, and negative behavior won't make you any friends in the thriving community. There truly is an audience for everything; you simply must market yourself honestly so the correct people find you, and be good to your listeners so they keep coming back.

Joining the realm of podcasters is enticing—we know, we were lured in too. But if you are considering it, we recommend that you sit down and think it through thoroughly before committing yourself. As much as it might be volunteer work, if you want to succeed it will be tantamount to having a full-time job. Ask yourself questions: Who is my dream audience? What will my show contribute to the medium that isn't already being done? Am I willing to have significantly less free time? How will I handle both the praise and criticism that comes with being a creative figure? Am I willing to invest in website and audio hosting for a podcast that might or might not ever make money? These are important things to consider that will help you avoid needlessly joining the podcasting graveyard.

There isn't a day when we aren't on call, because our "office hours" never stop. Even on vacation in Disney World with her children, Elizabeth has fielded texts about listener issues and administration necessities; while Christine once wrote an episode as she sat in her car before work so that we did not miss an air date when one of our hosts pulled out at the last minute. In addition to being independent scholars, through *Footnoting History* we have turned into businesswomen, working diligently to develop a reliable brand that delivers education and entertainment. We get to do fun things like collaborate on T-shirt designs but we also have to spend tedious hours creating pins for Pinterest. We often seek advice from people with more experience (like our parents) and have been known to quote *Shark Tank* now and again. Prior to *Footnoting History* neither of us had managed employees or given interviews, but these are normal things for us to do now.

We have also become more than medievalists. It's entirely possible that if we had remained in academia we would have carved out niche specialties and forever worked within their parameters. With *Footnoting History*, we have to constantly educate ourselves about new countries, times, themes, and people. Many of our listeners don't even associate us with our medieval origins, although we certainly have a high number of episodes about the Middle Ages. According to listener feedback, Elizabeth, in attempting to learn more about her adopted city of Atlanta, has found a second specialty: African American history. Through episodes about Black cemeteries and the civil rights movement, our listeners began to identify her with themes vastly different from those in her dissertation. Embracing her lifelong love of the Bonaparte clan and leading a series on France's revolutionary eighteenth and nineteenth centuries has established Christine as our resident Napoleonic authority. Every episode we do is an opportunity to further our growth as historians and indulge in exploring what interests us the most.

Working in an academic field but outside of the traditional pathway forces you to be creative to maintain your networks and access information, but if you do that then you can find your own special place in the community. Podcasting has given us the best of all worlds, allowing us to maintain our scholarly presence, expand our areas of expertise, hone our business skills, and educate the public. For many people we are the first point of entry into historical topics. They turn to us when a period drama piques their interest in a time period or figure. They choose us as their teachers because they like our methods and personalities, which is highly flattering. Although it has been a long journey and we may not have university affiliations, we think our younger selves would be proud about how we are fulfilling our historian dreams.

NOTES

1. Nell Frizzell, "'I Felt Like Morse Tapping His First Code'—The Man Who Invented the Podcast," *Guardian*, November 3, 2016, https://www.theguardian.com/tv-and-radio/2016/nov/03/christopher-lydon-podcast-inventor-open-source-mp3-files-interview. Brian R., "Infographic: Uncovering the True History of Podcasting," 2014, https://modicum.agency/blog/podcasting-infographic/. Charley Locke, "The First Podcast: An Oral History," *Wired*, September 1, 2017, https://www.wired.com/story/oral-history-first-podcast/.

2. Ben Hammersley, "Why Online Radio is Booming," *Guardian*, February 11, 2004, https://www.theguardian.com/media/2004/feb/12/broadcasting.digitalmedia.

3. *One Tree Hill*, episode 203, "First Day on a Brand New Planet," written by Terrence Coli and directed by Billy Dickson, aired October 19, 2005, on the WB.

4. *Oxford Dictionaries* (Oxford University Press), s.v. "podcast," accessed May 25, 2019, https://en.oxforddictionaries.com/definition/podcast. "Word of the Year: Frequently Asked Questions," *Oxford Dictionaries* (Oxford University Press), accessed May 25, 2019, https://en.oxforddictionaries.com/word-of-the-year/word-of-the-year-faqs.

5. "Ten History Podcasts You Need to Hear," CBC Podcast Playlist online, last modified October 6, 2015, https://www.cbc.ca/radio/podcastplaylist/ten-history-podcasts-you-need-to-hear-1.3259374.

6

An Independent Scholar of Art History outside the Academy and Museum

LAURA A. MACALUSO

Introduction

As an independent scholar, I don't want to blow up the academy and the museum, but I do want independent scholars and other creatives and professionals to have the opportunity to bring their special gifts to this important work. I want to see more collaborations forged among academics, community members, and others outside of the traditional sphere, with appropriate compensation. My academic training and professional background is in art history, a traditional field that has been less than supportive to independents. Thankfully, that is changing. In fact it is already happening in places near and far, and in many permutations—more than one can imagine. My own contributions through research, exhibitions, and publications across platforms (print and digital, academic and popular) have allowed me to meet and work with people across the spectrum of society whose work I find exciting and often inspiring, but there are plentiful frustrations and anxieties, too.

Art history, for almost all of its life, was—and remains—an academic discipline practiced by those in institutions of higher learning and museums. My thoughts, personal and reflective of more than twenty-five years involved with humanities practice, and specifically the discipline of art history, suggest that it is time for a reckoning. The changes in American society in the twenty-first century have been enormous, upending a long-held paradigm of the value and uses of such work, identity, and education in the academy. These changes include the impact of technology, the embrace of a "history from below" model for historians of all kinds, and a highly charged divide across culture and politics around the Atlantic world. Where does a practice such as art history fit into all of this, and in what ways can an independent scholar contribute positively to the enlightenment and encouragement of our seemingly difficult and diminishing world? This essay suggests there is room for the independent scholar to be a part of this work, participating in projects that are productive, satisfying, and needed. At the same time, independent scholars working with visual and material culture must grapple with the constant pressure of creating and finding work that works—meaning work that provides a financially sustainable life for them and their families, whatever shape that configuration may take.

There is nothing Pollyannaish about this. It is my reality and the likely reality for hundreds, if not thousands, of others like me. It is my contention that what I have been practicing on my own is a form of the academy-bound traditional version of art history, where a select few get doctorates, tenure-track jobs, and decades-long careers affording them equal amounts of pleasure (from teaching and research) and pain (from administrative chores).

Art history could benefit from the example of developments in our sister field, traditional history. Our historian colleagues recognized that their scholars and programs had a role to play outside of the academy and developed the practice of public history alongside their peers working in historic sites and museums and in community and economic development. Today public history has its own book series, journals, and teaching positions; art history—never as large as, and never as recognized by the public as traditional history—needs to do the same. A different path was paved by those arts administrators and a few scholars who created a field around the study and management of public art. Public art is a form of art-making that today is wide open in form, content, and placement, but what is needed are more public art historians— that is, those whose work is geared specifically toward working with the public in order to bring the critical thinking and even unique charms and idiosyncrasies of art history into meaningful, interesting, knowledge-producing community conversations.

One example of why a field called public art history is needed involves monuments, memorials, and murals. These public art incarnations require continued engagement by professionals in the face of continually arising challenges. Editorials, popular magazine articles, documentary films, and local committees debating these features of the public landscape often neglect to include the viewpoint of art historians, because, frankly, most people still don't know what art history is and what it can do for society. How many times have you heard about or attended a genuine community program—not a lecture—led by an art historian? This question is especially pertinent to people living outside of the country's most populous urban areas where the work of art historians is more plentiful. Art historians have something to say about all things visual and beyond, whether this is urban or rural, inside the museum or out, high culture or low, traditional or popular. This essay, then, recognizes people practicing art history outside the academy and the museum and offers thoughts on the ways in which public art history can engage with community.

Background: A Personal View of Art History in the Academy

I fell for art history around age nineteen or so, after having performed poorly in my first-year art history survey course. The professors were old, the slides were old, and my studying skills were shallow. I already had a proclivity for the visual arts as a young adult, which centered on reading books whose illustrations were easy to identify: Garth Williams in the Little House series, Edward Gorey in John Bellairs's Gothic/mystery books for young adults, and then of course Gorey's drawings for his own books, which I diligently copied instead of doing homework. In high school I had a few hands-on art classes at the local museum and won a few awards for my lame (but more competent than my classmates' efforts) art projects.

Art history settled on me hard in my second year at college. I don't exactly remember why—I wish I did. I was converted and the indoctrination has lasted. Perhaps it was that new, younger teachers came to the school, or that somehow I realized art history would literally bring me the world, sandwiched between a front cover and a back cover of big fat books filled with glorious works of art, mostly from Europe. My study skills, so lacking freshman year, got better. And then there was the realization that a full scholarship to my local state university was something to make full use of, and I began taking as many classes as I could, eventually graduating with a double major and a minor.

The concept of place, which would later become the bedrock on which I research and write, seeped into me not through academics, but by living in places that seemed to have lost their identities. Identities are often embedded in architecture or urban streetscapes or access to central spaces like libraries and museums, and all of these things were neglected, deteriorating, or altogether absent in the postindustrial Connecticut landscape where I was born and bred. Maybe my hyperawareness of the problems of the places where I happened to live and go to school pushed me toward this, but, as a subject, art history fit both interests perfectly. I knew there was plenty of art history around me—not in school and not in museums per se—but in the buildings, in the streets, in the cemeteries, in the parks, and in people's houses that I visited, houses and lives that were very unlike my own experience. Through art history I learned that the concept of place is related to placemaking—a way to understand and actively nourish a locale through community projects such as public art.

This education, this life, of course, all happened in the very last bit of the analog era, before social media, before the internet, and even before the ubiquity of personal computers. When I went to college at Southern Connecticut State University, my boyfriend had an electronic typewriter with a small removable hard black disk for saving documents. I think I may have borrowed it now and then to type papers. Halfway through college, SCSU opened a computer lab with big IBMs and sign-up sheets posted on the doors. So very much has changed in the academic humanities since that time that it feels like an ancient world, and art history, as a humanities discipline, has changed radically, too. But, the "digital turn" was slow to come to academic art history departments, indicating the tight reins held by academics who were trained by members of elite, prestigious universities, and whose own professors were solidly pre-digital twentieth-century people.

The professors whom I studied with, and later taught for, were adamant that PowerPoint slides were not going to replace the slides, Kodak carousels, and projectors that were the lifeblood of art history classes. The Art History department had a wall of black metal cases holding images on plastic slides, but there were even old glass slides in there, tucked in among the "newer" plastic slides. Each slide had handwritten notations across the top or side to identify the title and artist. Some slides had minuscule typed labels and a red dot made with a marker in the upper corner, to help load slides the correct way into carousels. Nothing was worse than standing in front of a class and having the next slide drop down—only to have the image upside down or backwards. Well, there was something worse, actually: a light bulb could burn out in the projector, which happened with such frequency that extra bulbs were always on hand.

For most of art history's life as a discipline, art historians concerned themselves with the visual arts, and specifically with the "fine arts," which included painting, sculpture, and architecture of the Western world. Other related materials, such as the crafts and decorative arts, were valued much less; only in small pockets might you find someone working on these materials in a professional environment, such as at a museum or historic house site or in classes taught by an adjunct lecturer who would never become full-time staff. Materials from non-Western cultures made their way into traditional art historical studies only via the perspective of the West.

Art historians had, for too long, been allowed to reinforce their own biases, not moving with the world outside, even when massive cultural change (the civil rights movement, women's rights, and gay rights, for example) created new forms of art that may or may not have made it into the museum.

That it took art history so long to catch up with demands from people from outside the academy may be a contributing factor to the lessening of importance with which American society treats the humanities and art history today. For all of these changes, outside of those few people who value, appreciate, and even love art history, most Americans still don't acknowledge or understand the practice of "learning to look" or the joy to be found in research, discovery, and interpretation of all those things that might fall somewhere under the umbrella of art history. This hit home in 2014 when President Barack Obama joked that students would have a better chance at getting good-paying jobs in the STEM fields, using art history as the subject against which manufacturing jobs and trade skills were compared. Ouch, Barry. The humanities and especially art history didn't need that.

The Humanities Inside and Outside the Academy and Museum

President Obama's remarks highlighted a long-running public discussion about the meanings and uses of the humanities to society, relevant especially to Americans, who have always been on a quest for monetary success through work production (make new things, sell new things, make money, repeat). Obama's quick dive into criticizing the humanities (while, at the same time, celebrating *Hamilton* at the White House) was nothing new. Questions about the purpose of pursuing the humanities abound in everyday media, and have for years. It's been widely reported that fewer and fewer college students are pursuing humanities degrees, and at the same time, many humanities programs are being reduced or cut altogether. Preceding this, for the past few decades, it's also been widely reported (and known, by those who spent years in the academic job market without success) that there are fewer and fewer full-time teaching positions available. In response, scholars and humanities administrators make the arguments that society needs people trained in the humanities and that, over the course of their lives, adults with humanities degrees earn as much as, and sometimes more than, those with STEM training. In the academic world, administrators have opened their tunnel vision to the fact that many of their graduate students will need, nay might even want, to pursue work outside of tenured teaching.

As noted, I've been an adherent of the study of art history since discovering the subject as an undergraduate at my local state university more than two decades ago. Since then, I've been in and out of schools to further my education and attain more degrees, while attending specialized academic programs and participating in and presenting papers at local, national, and international conferences. I've also taught college-level classes, published articles and books, and developed skills in grant writing while working for history, arts, and parks not-for-profit organizations. What I have seen from this vantage point is a slow but continuing shift in the way the humanities are taught in schools and presented to the public. But I have also noticed that these changes have been pushed from the outside, not the inside, confirming suspicion that the late twentieth century was overly committed to long-held established thought and teaching patterns for far too long. Most of my professors couldn't imagine a life outside of academia. It was all they knew, and for them, the pattern of graduate school and tenure-track (or, perhaps a curatorial position in a high-end art museum) had worked.

My own life and work are a reflection, and perhaps a result, of this much-changed professional work environment. With the turn of the millennium, 9/11, the Great Recession, and two new generations coming up in the educational system, some humanities-based academic disciplines began to open the door a sliver to allow for new areas of work—this includes the growing practice of public history, attached to history proper, which is arguably the "big man on campus" as compared to art history. Although related to history, art history is different. It is valuable, but in a humanities-challenged educational world, art history and what it offers can't really get anyone's attention unless it is hinged to a major institution and major money. Until very recently, art history usually made it into the news only when an exceptionally high-grossing work of art was sold at auction, or every few years when a possible new Leonardo came to light. But this is changing because those outside the academy and the museum are pushing against the authority held so tightly for so long.

I think this narrow authority was something I bucked against often over the decades, which likely led me to become an independent scholar without really understanding what I was doing or what the sacrifices would be along the way—and will be to the end of my life. I studied different disciplines within art history (Italian Renaissance in Florence for one master's degree from Syracuse University; European and American, nineteenth century, for more graduate-level studies at the Graduate Center, City University of New York) and ended up in a humanities program at Salve Regina University in Newport, Rhode Island, that allows students the flexibility to choose dissertation research that may be theoretical in nature or based on practical work experience. Even my dissertation adviser, who was attached to the Cultural and Historic Preservation Department, noted that I was doing something unique that didn't fit easily into what he, as a professor about to retire, knew about the field (of art and architectural history). Fortunately, he did not question the validity of the endeavor, and the dissertation project became *The Public Artscape of New Haven: Themes in the Creation of a City Image*, a book about the relationship between public art and city image. The work I did for the dissertation changed my life in the sense that putting together such a large research and writing project, and bringing it forward to completion and then publication, gave me the skills I rely on today. I write book proposals (I'm now working on another public art book for Wesleyan University Press) and craft grant proposals, which is a job that pays well, can be done with a flexible schedule, and keeps me connected to the arts and history organizations whose work I admire and believe important to society.

Art History Is Reframed by Changes to Society

Noted earlier, in addition to the changes wrought by the digital turn, society itself was moving on and out, demanding equality and equity in the presentation and conversation. Although there has been regressive movement thanks to a nationalistic, evangelical politicism in contemporary Congress, the #BlackLivesMatter and the #MeToo movements aren't going away. And in the academy and the museum, the demand for changes in the paradigm of who gets to collect material and write and present history is only growing stronger. Weekly there are headlines in the *Guardian*, the *Atlantic*, and the *New York Times* about world-famous museums on the hot seat for their lagging commitment to different communities on which their knowledge making resides. Examples of this include the British Museum—for holding on to the stolen Rapa Nui sculpture—and the Ottawa Museum in Canada, which is finally returning indigenous skulls after years of petition by native groups. In 2017 I had an experience with art history that helped to open my views to the ways in which independent scholars—or anyone wanting to work with museum-based materials outside of formal curatorial stature—can and do change the world.

That January, I noticed that two very different tours of American presidential portraits were being held on the same day, in the same city: Washington, DC, the capital of the United States since 1790. I was traveling from my home three and a half hours away in central Virginia to Connecticut, but I made a point of stopping in DC and taking both tours. The first was "The Brush Stops Here: Portraits of Presidents" at the National Gallery of Art on the Mall. The second was the Indigenous Corps of Discovery's tour of "America's Presidents" at the Smithsonian's National Portrait Gallery, a few blocks up from the Mall at the edge of Chinatown.

There is no way to compete with the collections of the National

Gallery, in terms of its portraits of presidents. The gallery has the first presidential painting done of George Washington and his family —his enslaved butler William Lee is there too—and also forty-seven Gilbert Stuart paintings. On the tour of the National Gallery, I learned something about the artists and their commissions, and a bit about the characteristics of the men who sat for their portraits— just as the kings and queens of Europe did, although with far less finery and fewer wigs. You might say that one version of the American story is embedded in these portraits; they depict ideas about the new country and its people—who they were, and what messages they were trying to send through their portraits. But what if we were to look at portraits of the presidents through the eyes of people who were completely left out of this story? As I learned on the next tour, it was possible to use portraits of presidents to track a very different history of the United States of America.

At the National Portrait Gallery, DeLesslin "Roo" George-Warren, a young man of the Catawba Indian Nation (South Carolina), greeted me at the life-size portrait of Andrew Jackson. George-Warren was granted an award from Humanity in Action to design "expeditions" that he calls the "Indigenous Corps of Discovery," taking on iconic American treasures such as presidential portraits or the National Park system to present a different narrative of people and places that are often considered icons of American history and culture. George-Warren's discussion in front of another portrait of Thomas Jefferson is a great example of resistance or political action used to call attention to injustice and point to a fuller understanding of history. Many people remember Jefferson as the author of the Declaration of Independence, while others remember him first and foremost as a hypocrite—a man who wrote significant words that covered personal inaction. Still others, especially Virginians, remember Jefferson for his famous house on the hill, which is shown on the reverse of the nickel.

George-Warren's tour went on to look at American presidents across the ages, up until the 1970s, the great era of civil rights activism. A portrait of Nixon by Norman Rockwell was a surprise, as was Nixon's pro-indigenous position. The tour then ended around the corner, at a huge portrait of Russell Means, the Native American actor and activist, whose renown earned him a colorful Andy Warhol treatment. I have been on many a museum tour, but rarely do museums hire folks from outside to be their educators. The Indigenous Corps of Discovery tour is a great example of why this should happen more often. I learned things about being a contemporary member of a tribe that I would not have learned from anyone else—even well-meaning, highly trained educators who study Native American history would not be able to articulate what it feels like to inherit and live indigenous identity every day.

Now, I see such interventions from the public happening at a quickened pace. George-Warren's actions changed the way I thought about not only presidential portraits but also who should be interpreting works of art and how there are very few opportunities to allow the public a way to do such work. This experience demonstrated that allowing outsiders in, in the long run, is a much greater way to remain relevant to society. The twenty-first century will surely not allow such walls to be built or maintained any longer. This stance is now replicated regularly in the critical discourse around museum collections across the Western world. As contemporary "Monuments Men" continue to track down, establish provenance for, and return works of art, artifacts, and books stolen by the Nazis, so, too, postcolonial countries on the African continent request the return of their material culture, as do Native American tribes under the Native American Graves Protection and Repatriation Act. And the country of Greece pushes, evermore, for the return of the Parthenon Marbles. This sort of work can and does happen in local communities, too. In

2019 I worked with the Lynchburg Museum, a city-owned entity, as it tried new techniques to address a highly charged "controversial" display of a Confederate flag.

An Independent Path

For my own art history work outside the academy and museum, I have focused much effort and interest on monuments, murals, and public art, and the ways in which these often publicly funded, publicly located materials shape our local, regional, and national communities. Little did I realize where this was headed fifteen years ago when I was starting this type of work. The monuments controversy is a good example of how little Americans recognize or use the expertise of art historians—most commentary about the Confederate monuments debate has been shaped by historians. Scholars of art history, who have inventoried, documented, and written books about public art, monuments, and memorials for most of the discipline's existence, have been left out. Maybe I and the art historians in the academy and museum with whom I studied or worked did not see the vitriolic public debate on the horizon because, being so far dug into the organizational aspects of the academy and the museum, we neglected to use these objects—out there, on the ground—in any significant way. And we neglected to connect with the many, many publics for whom these objects are either sacred commemorations or hurtful reminders of a past still present. Sure, I've done my share of student tours and trips to historic sites and landmarks, but a handful of site visits hardly makes up for the onslaught of the digital world and its ability to serve collective and political power through bold action. Younger generations, such as students on college campuses (for example, "Silent Sam" at the University of North Carolina, Chapel Hill), took their power out of the hands of higher education administrators and took down monuments themselves, tired of waiting for equity in the public realm to be given to them.

My work on monuments and public art ten or twenty years ago indicates that my tastes were already outside of the norm of art history. At the time, monuments were considered rather uninteresting and often banal, as compared to the fine art in museums, which generated the interests of the public, and of collectors whose deep pockets created a sensation every year at auction. Few people got excited about monuments then in comparison with today, when monuments seem to be in the news weekly. In between bouts of attending school for advanced degrees, I worked in a number of positions, beginning with the National Park Service (NPS). The NPS introduced me to collections management work and also to the twinned cultural heritage work present in all parks and historic sites, where balancing preservation and interpretation (nature and culture) is key to management practices. Although I was offered full-time work in the NPS, I turned the position down. From that time, I began a lifestyle of balancing my own interests in doing school and working, often at the same time, weaving in and out of cultural heritage work. Monuments became an area of interest because they were located in the public (often cultural in nature) and were more or less ignored by academia.

Because I'm interested in all things related to culture, I read across disciplines, a practice that enabled me to learn about opportunities for workshops, conferences, books, lectures, and festivals. I was fortunate to live for many years in New Haven, Connecticut, a small community enriched by a world-class university (Yale) and its museums (mostly free). I fed my head but also worked a lot, both as an art history adjunct lecturer in many of the state's public institutions of higher education and some private colleges and as a part-timer for organizations that dealt with nature and culture in some way, including parks departments and local historic houses/museums. While working for these New Haven entities, I began writing grants that funded projects that became exhibits and research, which were eventually shared in the digital realm (such as the inventory of public art of the City of New Haven, one of the first cities to upload to the Public Art Archive). All of this writing—whether for endless cover letters, grant proposals, administrative work, or scholarship opportunities—eventually, naturally, led to writing a dissertation at around age forty. For many folks in the working world, the coming of middle age means reaching a plateau of sorts. For me, it was more a moment of everything coming together, the dissertation and subsequent book a stamp of approval to some degree. I had already published two books during my years as a doctoral student—each was a stepping stone, getting me ready to try the "big thing" (the dissertation) and giving me insight into and practice in doing project management on my own. Not everyone who attends graduate school finishes, and the lack of support is one of the reasons for this. But with age comes confidence in your earned skills. That, plus the ability to persevere against those who say no, is central. When someone says no, I find another way.

Conclusion

Two community-based curatorial projects I worked on in 2019, which attempted to utilize the collaborative approach mentioned earlier, point to the very real limitations of trying to do this kind of work in a challenging system that is not designed for independent scholars.

The first was an exhibit of a unique community mural program, which ran for a few years in the late 1970s in New Haven. Part of the federal Comprehensive Employment and Training Act (CETA), this program was the first to offer people of color in the "Elm City" the chance to be both the makers of public art and the subject of public art. Although the project highlighted an important aspect of using art for community development and making identity, it was not supported by Connecticut Humanities; because there was no grant award, I myself had to pocket the costs for production of the large photographic images. The exhibit received a good review in the press, and the small amount of funding it would have taken to lessen the burden on an independent scholar is something that should be addressed. State humanities councils, supported by the National Endowment for the Humanities and by fundraising, are a major source for project funds. But, again, for those outside of a formal structure (either academy or museum), access to these funds is much more limited.

The second project was based in the community of Lynchburg, Virginia, where I have lived for seven years. This small city near the foothills of the Blue Ridge Mountains is a time capsule of "Lost Cause" mythology. Unlike more progressive Virginia cities such as Charlottesville and Richmond, in Lynchburg, home to the world's largest evangelical university in the world (Liberty, with more than 110,000 students), there has been no real agitation or discussion— yet—about the Confederate monuments that are situated around the city. Instead, most recently, a Confederate battle flag became the news; whether it should be put on display in the city museum was the subject of an intense conversation that has yet to find real movement forward, let alone resolution. Working with city museum staff, we attempted to create a "community platform" type of exhibit that would have been centered around the problem of displaying Confederate battle flag imagery. In the end, the Lynchburg Museum was not able to engage fully with this subject, due to political pressure. City of Lynchburg managers changed the shape and scope of the exhibit to emphasize the history of one particular flag in 1865 instead of examining the social ramifications and power the red, white, and blue pattern continues to hold on Americans.

Many young people whom I meet in my various jobs ask me how I created this role for myself. They don't use the words "independent scholar," and perhaps this is the crux of the thing. Most people see me as a contract worker or consultant, but, as an independent scholar, I see myself as someone able to enter into a variety of situations and contribute in meaningful ways, whether by asking critical questions, identifying resources, pushing boundaries, working with different people, and/or sharing ideas. I'm usually at a loss to sum up for the next generation how this all came together since I worked on these abilities to fit my personality. My skills are built around my strengths while avoiding the weaknesses (which I have learned over time is not really a great way to improve skills). But the truth is that I often work seven days a week, looking for opportunities, researching, and writing, while keeping one eye on my paid work. I have to learn the needs, desires, and working methods of separate organizations and bosses, as I try to keep everyone happy and ensure that grant deadlines are met. This work has brought me into contact with interesting people and places, and it continues to bear fruit, which makes student loan payments for the PhD easier to bear every month.

In 2019, I presented at two international conferences, two books were published (bringing my collection up to ten), one article was published, and two small exhibits were completed. But all of this is sometimes outweighed in my mind by the nagging thought that, as an independent scholar, I have not followed the pattern that most folks follow, that I do not have and will never have the same level of pay that others my age who work full-time jobs have, and that my future is basically unknown. I have struggled with this off and on for years but, thus far, keep coming back to this work, even as I know that as I get older, this will get harder. I have discovered the power of a power nap. Every year I hope that my health will hold out. I'm also hopeful that the United States will begin to see the error of its ways in this second Gilded Age, which offers little to nothing for most people but grueling work. Many people with whom I work look at me in envy, thinking to themselves that I have great freedom and that I am paid for what I do. Right at this moment, I'm writing a public art book, helping to create a mini exhibit about *The Negro Motorist Green Books*, collaborating with a partner on an "interpretation intervention" at a historic house museum, and preparing a grant application due next week. Of course, I am looking back at them with envy for their dependable paychecks, paid vacation time, and retirement accounts. The working world is not easy for anyone—not for those situated within systems or for those outside of systems. In 2020 it's hard to know where we are going as a society—even as a global society—but as an independent scholar I feel fortunate to have the tools to analyze situations, sift through information, and understand perspective during such a challenging moment of time.

PART THREE

FAMILY LIFE AND SCHOLARSHIP

7

Academia Didn't Have a Place for Me, So I Created My Own Academy

DANIELLE T. SLAUGHTER

When I look back to the moment I realized that my version of motherhood and the academy weren't going to mix, it came four years before I actually walked away. The moment that my boss uttered the words, "Maybe motherhood has changed you."

She said these words to me during a last-minute meeting held at her request. I sat across from her in silence with engorged breasts because it was time to feed my eight-month-old who was in a parking lot with my husband, waiting for me. I didn't know how to respond, so I just sat there and waited for her to finish chastising me for my attempts to not only engage my students in a creative manner but also balance the needs of my family.

What I really wanted to say in that moment was that of course motherhood had changed me, how could it not? This child had grown inside me for thirty-seven weeks. I'd spent three months trying to get him to properly latch in order to breastfeed without nipple shields. I was functioning on minimal sleep and trying to keep a human being alive. How could that not change me?

So, what was the offense that caused me to be called into the "principal's office," so to speak? *insert drumroll*

I was meeting with my students remotely every other Monday. I'll say that again: I was meeting with my students remotely *through the school's online platform* twice a month. I had not hidden this information from my superiors. It was in black and white in the syllabi that I was required to submit at the start of the semester.

So, why the outrage? I'd made the mistake of mentioning this technique in a professional development meeting. Yup, I shared with my peers that one way they could connect with their students via technology was by holding classes remotely. Apparently, someone started a rumor that I was just not holding class at all, and instead of asking me directly, my supervisor emailed me demanding to meet as soon as possible. She then sat across from me with every syllabus that I'd ever turned in during my teaching career and admonished me. Not once did she ask how it was working out with my students. She didn't give me an opportunity to discuss how much more participation I got from the quietest students with the remote classes. Or the fact that because I taught evening classes, this really helped my mostly nontraditional students because they didn't have to fight through traffic to get to class on time.

Nope, she told me how I was violating school policy, a policy that I didn't remember being informed of, by the way, and that I knew white male TAs violated without punishment because I had tutored their students in the past. She blamed it on my new role as a mother. Oh, and for good measure, she asked me who approved my right to use a novel in my composition class. Apparently, even though I was using the required text, I needed to have supplemental texts approved as well. Something else that was news to me since in the past the only time we needed approval was for our main text.

As I sit here typing this memory, I can feel myself getting angry all over again. But not with her. Nope, I'm angry with myself. I should've spoken up. I should've explained that I'd decided to theme my course on postapocalyptic America and that having my students read the then very popular novel, *The Hunger Games*, made for incredibly rich discussions on persuasive writing. That for the first time in a long time, my students were excited about arguing their versions of what life might look like in the future.

More than anything, I wish I had defended my choice to hold class remotely as a means of balancing my family life as well. I'd found a way to teach class while taking care of my child and also supporting my husband, who needed those two Mondays a month to attend an evening seminar for his teaching certification. And I was doing it well . . . my students were happy and thriving. My son was adjusting to my work life better.

As a Black woman, I've watched plenty of women balance work life and their families, so why should I be any different? I could make this work and still be a great wife and mother. My husband and I had both started preschool at age three. Prior to that we were always with family members when our mothers worked. Since we didn't have grandparents here, we'd decided that he'd continue his teaching career during the day, while I stayed home with our son. Then in the evenings I would teach for the first three years of our son's life, after which, I'd hopefully be done with my PhD (spoiler alert: I wasn't) and head out on the local job market.

And while this seems like a simple enough plan, we both knew that it would require sacrifice and less sleep on my part. I spent the first year of motherhood buried in cloth diaper laundry, composition pedagogy, and Black feminist theory texts. A week after we celebrated his first birthday, I took my comprehensive exam—a seven-day take-home exam combining my primary and secondary focus areas. There was very little sleep but I passed and that's all that mattered.

Academia was never my dream per se. If I'm being 100 percent honest, I didn't even know that this was in the realm of possibility until the fourth year of my undergraduate studies (I finished in five). As a first-generation college student, there were four career paths that I heard people discuss—medicine, engineering, teaching, and law. Tenth-grade geometry ruined my engineering dreams, which were based on my older cousin's job choice. While I was a natural at science, I found it boring, and being a doctor just didn't seem like my thing. I didn't like kids so teaching was out. So, I set my eyes on being a lawyer and one day becoming the first Black woman on the Supreme Court. Overachiever, much?

My initial law school dreams were dashed after I took a practice LSAT and realized that I would rather walk over fiery hot coals if it meant I didn't have to endure that level of torture again. I knew that I would have to ace my LSATs to even be considered for law school because my undergraduate GPA was tragic. I called my uncle in tears, and he reminded me how much I'd been enjoying my upper-level English courses, particularly the ones about rhetoric and social movements. We decided that I should go talk to my professor and discuss options. I went to office hours and that moment is when I learned about graduate programs in English. After talking to my uncle again, we decided I would apply for MA programs in English with a rhetoric focus, and then I'd apply for law school. At this point, I was in my last year of undergrad and scrambling for the future, so we found programs in Atlanta where I wanted to move and chose two with later application deadlines, so I could cram for the GRE. Miraculously, I was accepted into both programs, albeit provisionally for one. I accepted the university with the stronger rhetoric program, and started graduate school in the fall of 2006 with one goal—improve my GPA for law school.

A year and a half into the program, I received a fellowship to teach freshman composition, and everything changed. I remember calling my uncle two weeks into teaching my first class and practically screaming, "This is what I'm supposed to be doing. I love it. How can I become a college professor?" It was the first time I've ever felt like this is the work I'm supposed to do with my life and it's a way for me to still change the world in some way.

I can't ever say that I loved graduate school. I can say that I loved parts of it—the reading and discussions mostly. It was amazing to be around so many other people who didn't just read a book at face value. However, I wasn't prepared for how lonely I would still feel during the process. For starters, I was younger than many of my classmates and I was Black. While I was accustomed to being the only Black person in classes from my undergraduate studies, I was not used to having very little contact with other Black students in similar positions. There wasn't a dorm or cafeteria for me to find the other Black people like I could in undergrad. Add in the fact that I'm an introvert and not much of a drinker, so I often felt awkward attending social functions. I won't say that any of my classmates were blatantly racist, but there were definitely times when I didn't know how to explain the energy I felt from them. I now know that I was experiencing microaggressions and implicit racial bias.

Additionally, I found it difficult to connect with faculty, which is a huge part of graduate school as well. I didn't know that I was supposed to reach out to faculty in order to find a mentor or that I needed to attend these social events in order to meet them outside of class. I was still very much operating under my undergrad policy of going to class, doing my work, and staying out of trouble. I did eventually find mentors thanks to a professor realizing I had attended her alma mater for undergrad when I inquired about a tutoring position in the writing studio. However, as a first-generation college student, I had no idea what I had gotten myself into when I entered the ivory tower.

This loneliness would serve as a foreshadowing for my life as a graduate student mother.

I continued teaching for four more years after that unfortunate incident, only leaving when my graduate funding ended. While I didn't attempt the online remote classes anymore, I continued to engage with my students in other unconventional ways. For starters, I opened up to them about the nonacademic specific writing I did on my website, Mamademics, a website I initially started in January of 2012 while pregnant to chronicle my life as an academic and first-time mother.

Mamademics actually started because of peer pressure. One of my online friends was working on a website about celebrity motherhood. She asked me to guest post as a "real" mom. The first post I wrote was so well received that she convinced me to start my own blog. She actually walked me through all the steps of purchasing a domain and hosting. Oh, and she helped me come up with the name. At the time, I thought it would just be a place for me to track my life—like a more official Xanga journal. I didn't even use my real name for the first year.

I showed my students how I used rhetorical strategies to discuss current issues that plague our country. I even let them see the backlash I received online. I encouraged them to use their own lives in their writing. We talked about what they were reading, watching, and listening to beyond academia. I asked about their struggles and battles. My classroom became a space for both group therapy and writing.

Showing my students the writing not only transformed my teaching but it also led to what I now affectionately call Mamademics Academy. It was during one of our classroom discussions where I showed how I was using pathos and logos to help white mothers see why they needed to care about murdered Black children. My students learned the ways that words can sting while also pushing to action. It also led to the theme of needing parents (and teachers) to be more truthful.

One of my students mentioned that I should teach a class, and I remember laughing when she said it. And then she mentioned that she was serious because everything I'd been teaching them about the realities of the "American Dream" startled them, and they wished their parents or teachers had been more truthful. I remember thinking that their parents weren't deliberately teaching them the wrong thing. From what I'd learned hearing from parents after viral posts, many of them either just didn't know the truth or didn't know how to effectively explain it to children. Suddenly, creating my own class didn't seem like such a joke anymore.

I used what I learned teaching freshman composition at the collegiate level to create an online course for parents, "Raising an Advocate: 101—Exposing the Three Ps: Privilege, Prejudice, and Pride." The initial course launch was slow at first. But then in the summer of 2016, police killed Alton Sterling and Philando Castile, and everything changed. I was able to use my research in pedagogy and Black feminism to create a course that was accessible to parents no matter their educational background. I even included some of the supplemental readings I'd used in the past to teach my students about privilege and prejudice, such as "Explaining White Privilege to a Poor White Person." Those long-forgotten online discussion boards were transformed into Facebook group discussions that I was able to facilitate while taking care of my son.

The response to my course was so overwhelming that I've since made it into a self-paced-only option because it became too hard emotionally to facilitate the courses in real time. Allowing my emotions to play a role in my work would definitely be frowned upon in the ivory towers of academia, but in the online space it's made me a more authentic influencer. I never intended for Mamademics to become a school of sorts. The initial goal was to create a space for academics who were mothers to feel less alone; however, it became clear that parents everywhere needed an educational space to help raise children who would change the trajectory of the world.

Mamademics Academy became a space for parents to learn not only how to have difficult conversations with their children but also how to have those conversations with themselves. More importantly, it became a space for building community. Unlike academia, this was a space that did not make you feel stupid for not knowing "correct" terminology. You weren't given a list of reading and expected to dissect it alone. No, in Mamademics Academy, everyone learned from one another, and I tried my hardest to make sure all the language was accessible. I took the time to break down academic concepts in a way that anyone could understand because intellectual elitism is not going to help fix the problems in our world.

More importantly, I focused on creating a space where people didn't feel like they were in this alone. We were all participating in the raising of children, either our own or as part of a larger village. It was totally okay to bring your whole self into Mamademics Academy and not just the version the public wanted to see. I didn't want anyone to feel isolated in the same ways that I was experiencing in the academy

The isolation I felt as a first-time mother in academia was not only painful but was detrimental to my mental health. I went from seeing classmates in the library for writing and study dates to being home alone reading for comprehensive exams while nursing a baby. By the time I entered campus for teaching, everyone else was either already gone or leaving. Our department was literally *closed*, so I had to use my key to make copies "after hours."

The loneliness wasn't just from being on campus all alone. It was a result of suddenly no longer being included in out of school activities either. I'll be the first to admit that I did not always accept invitations to social events—sometimes because I'm an introvert and sometimes because I know that my invite was a mere afterthought once my presence in a space was noticed. However, almost all of those invites ceased the moment I became a mother. And my messages reaching out to invite people over for lunch or studying were often ignored. I tried not to pay it much attention until I started to notice how white women who became pregnant were treated. Suddenly, there were huge baby showers for them, organized by faculty, no less. I'd see pictures on social media of single classmates visiting new moms and hanging out with them socially. So, they didn't ignore my invitation to my kid's first birthday party because it was a kid's party, they ignored it because it was *my* kid's party.

It's hard to admit that this liberal space simply saw me as another Black woman with a baby and every stereotype that comes with it. The invisibility that I tried to ignore for years became so damn clear once I was no longer the Black scholar who sacrifices everything for the academy. I was no longer available to take extra tutoring hours or volunteer to sit at tables for bake sales. I wasn't always in my on-campus office working, which meant that I was no longer seen but not heard. I didn't have the means or the desire to put my child in day care for eight hours a day, which meant I couldn't possibly be serious about my career anymore.

If they had taken the time to really talk to me, they would've known that I was even more committed to my career than in the past. I not only had a child to provide for from a monetary standpoint but I was on a mission to show my young son that women belong in any space they want to occupy. I didn't say no to the academy because I put motherhood first. The academy said no to me because I wanted motherhood and scholarship to coexist.

What can the academy do to help future Black mothers in graduate programs? First, they need to figure out how to support their Black students, period. Second, they need to come up with a plan for students who become mothers. Our identity is talked about in hushed tones or as a joke to make white people feel more comfortable. And honestly, it's not my job to come up with that plan for them, unless they want to pay me. However, I will give this freebie—*Hire Black women faculty! Hire mothers!* Talk about your program's commitment to your scholars having a well-rounded life outside the ivory tower.

Once they've figured out these two things then they can move toward helping Black mothers in the academy. As of now, most universities do not have a clear system in place for graduate students of color. There are no clear policies for how graduate mothers must be treated. Everything is decided by your department, which can frequently change based on who is in charge. For example, I watched two of my colleagues have children prior to myself and then be allowed to opt out of some of the "mandatory training" sessions, which really was mostly review for those of us who had been on staff for longer than two years. When I had my child, I wasn't allowed to miss that training. I sat in a two-day mandatory training with a five-month-old exclusively breastfed child who ended up vomiting all over me by the end of the second day. And not one thing that we covered was new to me, but the person in charge told me I had to be there. Over the next few years, I would frequently bring my child with me to these mandatory training sessions because my husband worked during the day and there's no way I could afford child care on the meager stipend we received. Even when he started preschool, I still ended up bringing him with me because he only went for half a day and all the meetings were typically in the afternoons. Initially, bringing my child to these things gave me pause. But they knew I was a mother, and I wasn't going to hide that to make anyone else feel comfortable.

If the academy wants to stop losing some of their most brilliant scholars, they need to realize that their scholars' identities matter.

Many of us are no longer willing to sacrifice who we are in order to fit into the mold academia has created. What makes the community I've built with Mamademics so successful is the fact that I expect identity to matter. I know that we all bring so many different layers of ourselves into the space, and I never expect anyone to hide one of them. Instead, I challenge my community to consider the role our different identities play in how we parent, and how we can use them to our advantage. I've literally taken what we learn about scaffolding in pedagogical theory courses and used it when helping parents navigate race and social justice.

The absolute best part of sharing my story and building Mamademics has been the connection with other academic moms. Specifically, finding other Black women in the academy who were going through similar situations provided a sense of community. It also helped me realize how much more enriching the academy would be if they allowed scholars to show up as their whole selves. There are only so many ways you can interpret the texts of dead white men, but when you allow scholars to bring their life to the work, you realize that they are the future of the canon. Black women who can apply feminist theory to Beyoncé's *Lemonade* help spark a new generation of scholars. But maybe that's what the academy is scared of—if they allow us to be our whole selves, everyone will realize that old white men should no longer be at the helm of the ivory tower.

If I had been asked to write this essay in 2013, I'd have said, sure, I'm an independent scholar. Everyone in academia is an independent scholar. The system is set up in a way that forces us all to work independently. From our coursework to our exams to our thesis or dissertation, we might have a committee guiding us, but we're still doing this work independently. However, we are all dependent on the university to validate our work. Our independence is an optical illusion covered in course requirements, exam lists, approval signatures, and university ownership. In 2019, being an independent scholar has an entirely different meaning for me. I'm an independent scholar because I'm choosing what I read. I'm choosing what and when I write. I'm choosing how I educate my audience. I'm choosing the projects that I take on and the work that I want to do.

My work with Mamademics has opened up so many other doors when it comes to my career. In 2017, a viral post I wrote about the dangers of online mommy groups for mothers of color led to me signing with a literary agent days before going into labor with my second child. At the time of this publication, I'm working on a book proposal that is part childhood memoir, part parenting manual for Black moms.

In addition, I am currently part of the leadership team for Mothering Justice, a nonprofit organization based in Michigan. Mothering Justice empowers mothers to influence policy on behalf of themselves and their families, by dedicating their work and programs to returning the power of decision making to the ones impacted by these decisions the most. I became a part-time employee for the organization in 2019, but I've been doing freelance consulting work with them since 2017. Since the nonprofit's offices are in Michigan, I work remotely and check in during staff meetings or planned in-person meetings throughout the year.

At present, I am the lead facilitator for Mamas' University, an online fellowship geared toward Black moms and other moms of color in America. The fellowship focuses on helping mothers with interpersonal activism, specifically, in the digital sphere, health care, schools, and their own homes. We do not focus on only one issue because we know that mothers don't lead single-issue lives. As lead facilitator, I manage the other speakers that we bring in for seminars; create most of the curriculum we use; and help bring a group of moms together as one unit. I also created the application process for 2020 and will be responsible for picking the fellows from the applicants received.

The isolation created in academia prepared me for working in an independent remote environment. I knew what it was like to be provided with a task and a deadline but not have someone actually making sure I worked on the task every day. The theories I studied in regard to feminist pedagogy and composition pedagogy gave me the expertise I needed to create curriculum for Mamas' University. My experience teaching freshman composition taught me the classroom management skills needed to run an online fellowship with various personalities. I use the skills I learned in the academy every single day in my independent work life.

However, being sought out to join Mothering Justice's leadership team due to my expertise in building community with Black mothers, as well as my unique style of teaching, came about because of Mamademics. Signing with a respected literary agent came about because of my writing on Mamademics. Even being included in this anthology came about because of what I've built with Mamademics.

As empowering as it is to say that I've created a body of work that stands alone outside of the academy, there is also a part of me that so badly wants to be included in the traditional conversation of scholarship. I would be lying if I tried to pretend that I do not battle with insecurity from not having a PhD after my name. I've watched many of my classmates finish their degrees, and each time I feel this twinge in my chest. I know that this twinge comes from wanting to make sure I'm taken seriously by my peers for the work I do. It's also from wondering if I made the right choice to focus on my family and chart my own path in terms of career. Charting your own path is rocky and insecure. There is no one to blame but yourself if things don't work out. However, there's also no one squelching your creativity or creating arbitrary rules with no regard for the humans who need to carry them out.

I do hope that I will be able to at least finish my degree even if I never end up a tenured professor. Not because of prestige, but because I don't like quitting things. I also don't want my children to feel like they are the reason I didn't finish my degree. Oh, and all this student loan debt needs to be worth something. I'm honestly not sure what finishing the degree will look like since, in the meantime, the mentor I mentioned earlier has moved on to another university. I appreciate her giving me a list of what to do once she left but I still haven't followed through with it. If I'm honest, I'm just scared to be rejected by a potential new dissertation chair. I know that I need to be in the right mental space when I do finally take that plunge and I definitely want my youngest child to be in school, so that he's afforded the same attention that his older brother received. I'm also hopeful that going back after establishing a name for myself outside of the academy will mean more support from the department. It's my hope that they will see how being my whole self is leading me to create my own empire of sorts and that they will allow me the freedom to be that person in my dissertation as well.

No matter what happens in the future, I am incredibly proud of the fact that my current work isn't validated by a university name behind it. I don't sign my work with any university name next to it, as I'm currently on hiatus from my PhD program. My work stands alone. People read it because it has Mamademics behind it. A brand that I created and built with the bricks from the tower of isolation that the academy built around me.

8

Burn It Down: From Adjunct to University Staff to Stay-at-Home Mom to Beauty School

KATHERINE ANDERSON HOWELL

When approached to write this chapter, I hesitated at first. Other than a phrase to put in place of an institution in bios and on conference name tags, I did not necessarily always identify with the label "independent scholar." The family and economic pressures present in my life caused leaving higher ed, in many ways, to be a choice made for me. On reflection, however, I acknowledge consciously making the choice to continue to research, write, present, and maintain a consistent scholarly presence. The fandom studies, pedagogy, and disability studies work that I do provides as much meaning to my life as motherhood and poetry. Kelly J. Baker has pointed out that "women, especially mothers, are expected to sacrifice ourselves—our desires, aspirations, bodies and even lives—to keep others happy. There are social and cultural expectations (and rewards) for mothers to appear as martyrs, who serve others and never themselves. Women's labor goes unnoticed and unpaid because our labor makes the system run."[1] I refused to be a martyr to academic institutional life, thus subverting those social expectations. And, as a stay-at-home mom, my brightly colored hair and writing career also defy the expectation of sacrifice. The path toward creating an intentional, active, independent scholarly life involved a great deal of searching. It still does, but now it searches with less concern for the values of disinterested institutions.

For eleven years after I graduated with my masters in English, I taught college composition as an adjunct at a variety of institutions. At Boston College, my alma mater and where I learned to teach composition, I taught first-year writing in a seminar-style course where I had control over the syllabus and assignments. At Massachusetts College of Pharmacy and Health Sciences, to which I often commuted in a taxi between classes at Boston College, I taught more of a traditional, research-based composition course, including "developmental" courses with blue book exams graded anonymously, twice, by me and another professor.

In Boston, I learned to teach different demographics: wealthier students at Boston College, and working- to middle-class students at Massachusetts College of Pharmacy and Health Sciences. I worked another job, an administrative job at my church, while teaching at these two schools. I urgently needed three paychecks; I had begun paying back my loans as soon as I graduated. I did not seek an income-based deferment, out of fear I would never get out from under the principal; after all, in the United States the majority of student debt is owed by women.[2] This choice, and the resulting budget, as well as my exhaustion, cost us friends—none of my husband's law school friends worked paid jobs. The only reason I did pay off my loans? My husband's bonuses later in life.

When my husband and I moved to Jackson, Mississippi, for a year for his federal clerkship, I taught at both Holmes Community College and Hinds Community College. At Holmes during the fall and spring semesters, I taught night and Saturday classes to nontraditional students. Some felt threatened by being taught by someone younger than them, to the point of one student asking to go home early to make meat loaf because her children did not know how to make it. Telling a fifty-year-old woman that "meat loaf does not constitute an emergency" is among my favorite teaching stories. Some students felt they could share their intimate problems, like their tears over abortions; and some conspired with me to break campus rules so that they could finish the course.

This was before the days of viral images of the kind professor teaching while holding a student's fussy baby, but these viral images demonstrate how desperately campus child care is required, both for students and for professors. It may be more difficult for female academics to get full-time faculty positions, tenure-track positions, or staff positions with the flexibility needed to care for their children (or even with enough pay to cover the astronomical cost of child care). I refused to put my students' degrees in jeopardy. I allowed one student to bring her child along to attend class until the second time security caught us. At that point, we struck a deal—if she turned in her work electronically and came to class for the first ten minutes—the college had a strict attendance policy because of state funding requirements—I'd pretend to not see when she slipped out. She earned a good grade and graduated on time. Baker asks, in arguing for women's unruliness as a path to liberation, "Behaving well appears to be the only way to get ahead, but is it worth it?"[3] My student and I would answer, no. It is not.

At Hinds during the fall and spring, I taught four different levels of composition: "remedial," "developmental," Comp One, and Comp Two. All had preset syllabi, and I began to learn to negotiate disability issues. Many of the students in remedial and developmental courses had diagnosed and undiagnosed learning and cognitive differences. I also learned how to beg forgiveness rather than ask permission regarding how to teach students when the presets did not meet the needs of these students with disabilities and differences. In the summer at Holmes, when I taught Comp One and Two, and American Lit One and Two, I negotiated the culture clashes between the primarily white students who usually attended private, four-year colleges and were taking the classes for transfer credit, and the primarily Black students who usually attended the community college. I began to learn how to thoughtfully use white privilege to advocate for my Black students. These skills of unruliness are essential for white teachers to have. Hammond reminds us that "some colleges truly are life-transforming, at least in the economic realm" for marginalized and poor students and that those of us who can teach them without burnout need to do so.[4]

But burnout, for contingent faculty, seems impossible to avoid. In Mississippi, I taught at multiple schools, taught six days a week, and taught five courses at a time. I supported my husband, then a law clerk, with enormous tolls on my mental health from the stress. Baker puts it best: "Women's happiness has never been guaranteed, but women's suffering appears to be."[5] During this year, my beloved grandfather died. Family dysfunction from my in-laws plagued me as well.

My back ached from lugging a bag of grading and books, or from hours driving on the road. I would commute for an hour each way in a 1999 Jeep Cherokee, carrying hundreds of papers at a time. Grading developmental and remedial papers took intense focus, as the syllabi required nightly homework and specific kinds of marks. As we only had one car, I had little time to rest. I had to drop my husband off, drive an hour to my 8 a.m. class, pick my husband up, then get to my 6 p.m. class. I knew, in my body, what Katie Rose Guest Pryal means when she says that adjunct work can break one's back.[6]

When we settled in DC, I only did the road scholar gig for one semester. I taught at both American University and George

Washington University once. Then I received a part-time contract, with union benefits, health benefits, and retirement benefits at George Washington University, so I chose to focus on one school. At George Washington University, I could set my own theme and control my own syllabi, although I still taught composition.

Still, my own writing, creative and scholarly, suffered. Because I only held an MA, and because I knew I did not want a PhD, I lacked clear scholarly models. I lacked connection to graduate school mentors, in part because of my lack of interest in a PhD, and in part due to my mental health. I did not know of any formalized alumni support network for research or scholarly growth. It might have existed outside of my sphere. Because graduate school can focus so much on one discipline, those of us with inter/multidisciplinary interests may not easily fit. My anxiety and issues with extended family complicated the connections I did have.

Over the years, I started and dropped many projects, and had no clear sense of where to publish or when. I had the false sense that poetry and scholarship existed at odds with each other; one could not and should not produce in multiple genres. Not entirely sure what I wanted or what options existed, I knew that I was tired and overworked, and the mental and physical pain only seemed to increase.

At George Washington University, I began to do research for a class about adapting *Jane Eyre*. I approached Kathy Larsen for help, and I often joke that I forced her, much more of an introvert than I, to be my friend and mentor. The University Writing Program at GWU gave me the ability to walk into someone's office for guidance. Kathy, and others in the program, provided me with the encouragement that my work was a viable scholarly direction worth pursuing.

This scholarly direction, fandom studies, took me to the national conference of the Popular Culture Association in 2014, where my presentation led to two important things. First, it ended up published as an article in *Pennsylvania English*, and second, it caught the attention of an editor from the University of Iowa Press. I had the opportunity to edit my first collection, *Fandom as Classroom Practice: A Teaching Guide*, published in 2018. Along with Joe Fruscione, I found my way as a passionate advocate for adjunct rights, working with both the adjuncts in my program and the Service Employees International Union (SEIU), which represented George Washington University adjuncts.

Still, the grind wore on me. I parented two small children. An entire genre of essay discusses the graduate student or professor with children, mostly focused on the delights. Kyle Sebastian Vitale writes of how academia and family life work together; this is a beautiful sentiment until we remember that in higher education women require more education than men to achieve equal pay and that there is a higher service load expected of women.[7] Pryal reminds us that higher education expects more of women and provides less career satisfaction.[8] Motherhood, in the academy, carries with it the responsibility of carving out the space and time required. I, as an adjunct, had to deal with my male office mate— who had been given my pumping schedule in writing via email— loudly complaining that I could not hog the office when he needed it. He had never bothered to share his office hours, or post them. I had literally never heard from him before. Thankfully, the full-time faculty member across the hall went on maternity leave, and gave me the key to her office so I could pump in there.

On top of parenting, I battled administrative messes. Somehow, someone in HR or payroll or contracts accidentally terminated me during my second pregnancy. Rather than providing me with unpaid maternity leave as with my first pregnancy, my contract was terminated. The person on the phone promised the office coordinator who told me this news that I would be rehired in a subsequent semester; she did not clarify whether it would be under my current contract at the current rate. I hired a lawyer, and my administrators fought for me (I cannot speak highly enough of the advocacy and support of the leadership of the University Writing Program regarding this issue). But at eight months pregnant and high risk, I did not need stress and upset at the end of a semester. While the issue was resolved in my favor, I never did get the paperwork promised from the provost reinstating me. My status just changed in the system from "terminated" to "active."

Each new semester would include pay issues for me or other adjuncts. Parking errors were also an issue. Once, my union rep mansplained basic math to me over email as a way of downplaying the importance of these errors; he felt the concerns of the adjuncts on his campus were far more important. These are all just part of what Pryal calls "the small daily humiliations" of adjuncting.[9] And I was lucky—very lucky. Yes, I was part of the academy; yes, I got to write and work with great students and colleagues. Yes, I had a union, which had won me access to health insurance and a retirement benefit. But after over a decade of teaching composition, and after years of dealing with humiliations like this, I wanted a change.

When a career development position came open at the Disability Support Services office at George Washington University, I leapt at the chance to become full-time staff. At the interview, the director provided me with examples of other employees who worked from home once a week, assured me how flexible my schedule would be, and told me how quickly my advancement would move forward as I gained experience. She also assured me that I would be salaried. The director had no control over whether my position was salaried. That was for HR to decide based on mysterious criteria, and the turnover in HR was rumored to be high, making my hiring process slow. I was hired as an hourly employee.

Getting hired was an ordeal, and took weeks. I protested at first by sitting at home, refusing to come in. Ultimately, though, I chose to take what was offered despite multiple go-rounds with HR via email. As a person with multiple chronic pain conditions and diagnosed anxiety and depression disorders, I thought it could be important for students to connect with someone with whom they might identify, like the graduate student with disabilities who had held the part-time version of the position before me. College student bodies have become more diverse; women hold a slight majority. Faculty do not necessarily reflect this diversity, and staff do not either.[10] Disabled students nationwide make up about 10 to 11 percent of the undergraduate student population.[11]

When I started, I had recently received epidural injections into my spine to attempt to mitigate a severely herniated disc that was causing horrific pain. This meant that I organized my three-way shared cubicle in such a way that my computer monitor was high, my chair was low, and my back faced the hallway. Other staff members treated my shared cubicle, and other cubicles, as public space; meetings with students, which should have been respected as private, were interrupted to get to files in drawers and containers. Old, unarchived files stored in my cubicle got messy to the point that I had to reorganize them, and someone once slammed the file containers so hard on my cubicle desk that my computer monitor bounced. She did not acknowledge my presence. When those of us who worked in the cubicles asked for more respect for our space, our supervisor, poor exhausted guy, told us it was not a battle worth fighting.

When I sought out the promised work from home time from my supervisor, he told me that I never should have been offered that at all. I held a "student-facing" position; even when students were not on campus, I was required to be. Pryal argues for a cessation of the notion that women have to overperform, and wear ourselves thin in order to succeed.[12] I wore myself thin that summer in DC. The air conditioner in our office worked poorly when it worked at all. The office was routinely eighty-eight degrees. I listened to a coworker talk on speakerphone all day while I met every goal I set for the quarter, created new ones, and met those. I drove to two different pickups twenty minutes apart to get my children after it all.

I discovered the worst of the failed promises when my director told me that the "flexibility" I expected, needed, and that she had promised consisted of the ability to use sick leave each time I needed to take my son to his therapy appointments and to have a blind eye turned for the hour I slipped out for my own therapy once a week for a few months (although if it continued, I would have to formalize it as an accommodation). That hour was already deducted from my check as the lunch I rarely took. My child was disabled, as were the students we worked with, but there was a lack of compassionate treatment and support.

My director informed me that I could not take a quarter day of sick leave, even though that was all I needed. I could take eight hours, four hours, or none. That was "flexible": being allowed to use half or whole days of leave when I needed to use leave. I had to put all of this in writing in an email after a contentious meeting with my supervisor and the director, and I reminded my supervisor that I had kept notes on all the verbal offers. The false flags stopped after that, but my female director often asked me why my husband, by this time a partner in a law firm, could not take on more of these family responsibilities. She implied that there was a gender issue in my home that caused me to neglect my work duties. The gender gap in higher education allows some university leaders to hold outdated ideas about women's work/life balance. My home did not have a gender issue; it had an economic issue. My pay as an hourly university staff member did not compare to the pay and responsibilities of my husband, a law partner. My work, however, did have a gender issue. My family responsibilities and the perception that I lived a stereotyped life appeared to stall my advancement, although my director blamed HR. I wanted to move from hourly to salary, and get the benefits promised to me when I took the job.

I produced and worked creatively and efficiently, having created a program, complete with marketing, from the bare bones of what existed before. Baker states that "if a woman is to be understood as confident and/or influential at work, then she also must be liked."[13] I was confident and productive, and I connected well with students. I was also unruly, preferring to insist that things change, to ask why things needed to be a certain way, and to do what was best for students rather than to toe departmental lines. We know that "women must both work harder and be kinder than men to get ahead in their careers. Unruliness puts us at risk."[14] Ultimately, doing things my way, even though I did what my director asked for and more, irritated and confused her. Because of this, and likely because of my family duties as well, she told me that she did not understand how my work, especially the work I had done during her medical leave, had fulfilled my job duties. She made me, and only me, produce additional documentation for my annual review to prove that I had met metrics. When given this documentation, she stuck it in a drawer in front of me without looking at it. My supervisor, to whom I directly reported, gave me a glowing annual review. I began to realize I have a problem with authority, in particular the blindly wielded authority of the university.

However, I created a solid career development program: one of the first things I did was win a grant from the career services fund to create a professionally produced video introducing me and the program to students. By the time I left, I had created goalposts for how to work with students of each year and a variety of disability categories, relationships with multiple organizations on and off campus, and templates for students for cover letters, budgets, and other basic career skills. I developed supportive relationships with students: I helped them develop mantras to lower anxiety before and after interviews; sat with them to plan strategies for career fairs and business partnerships; and encouraged them as they worked through common insecurities that can be exacerbated by disability and difference. I used a survey to collect data and feedback about what our students needed and wanted from career development and then created programming accordingly. I even created a gender neutral, disability inclusive explainer about what "business dress" meant. I fielded phone calls from students encountering unexpected bumps in the road, and from alumni wondering how to ask for accommodations in their workplace. I reassured frightened parents whose children had been hospitalized or ill, and I hugged and shook hands with proud parents whose children had gotten great internships, first jobs, or grad school acceptances. I wiped tears, gave hugs, and, best of all, gave lots of congratulatory high fives. I worked on pushing disability into campus diversity programming by serving on the Diversity Summit Committee and by planning the first ever Disability Awareness Month, with a focus on intersectional connections. We featured Camisha Jones, a Black disabled poet; we screened *Murderball*, about wheelchair athletes; and we held multiple career events.

After a year of full-time university staff work, I had burned through my accumulated sick leave, even some vacation, and was considering taking Family and Medical Leave Act (FMLA) leave to care for my child with disabilities. The true irony is that FMLA would have made it possible for me to access the things I was promised in the first place: the ability to work from home, the ability to leave early without penalty, the ability to set a truly flexible schedule, and so forth. Even more ironic? I learned the ins and outs of FMLA in order to help my students and alumni as part of my job duties. I gave far more to the university than I received. The question became clear: What really defines support from an institution?

For one thing, institutional support should involve basic documentation of job duties and expectations for their execution. I was told to be creative and then felt punished when I was made to prove my creativity had filled the job duties. There should be recognition of accomplishments and real opportunities for funding for special and innovative projects. Staff and all faculty types need supported time for projects that forward the stated goals of the department. And the department should be clear on its goals. They should be achievable. All departments should provide clarity about the actual time expectations of the department. Parents, particularly parents of children with high needs, cannot always be on call for their departments. What matters most? Is it getting the forty hours in the office, or making sure that all the students have been seen and all the emails read? Gender and racial equity are not present yet. Disability equity is not present yet. Higher ed has work to do. Flexible use of leave time is an essential part of supportive institutions. I might have actually considered staying longer if I had been able to use my leave in a way that was actually flexible. Instead, I was given rigid rules that served only to eat up my time and back me into a corner. Paid family care leave is part of the flexibility needed for success.

My family situation demanded that something change, so I quit to become a stay-at-home mom. Again, the economics made it clear that I needed to be the one to do it, and I hated the situation I was in at the university. My job made me ragey. I walked away from poor physical, mental, and institutional working conditions. After I left, *Fandom as Classroom Practice* was published and did well. My poetry publications increased, as did my creative freedom: nearly one year after I quit, I was nominated for a Pushcart Prize. I wrote the book proposal for my second book.

My family's life became, slowly, more stable. I raise two children with high needs: one with severe allergies, and one with attention deficit hyperactivity disorder, which has required intensive interventions due to the resulting emotional dysregulation. My home has very strict food regulations. Everyone who enters our home and stays learns to use an EpiPen. My home has very strict parenting rules; we follow the principles of parent-child interaction therapy. Laminated occupational therapy slogans decorate our walls, and we have what on the surface appear to be absurdities, like an indoor wooden play structure with monkey bars and a slide, and an outdoor toilet in order to help our son stay regulated. My children sleep with aromatherapy and weighted blankets. Routine is everything.

My creative freedom comes at the price of having no breaks from family demands. I am always on call. My labor, indeed, "makes the system run" now. My children go across the street to school, and my workday ends when school ends. I work from home, and part of my job involves basic household chores. My family's stability comes at the cost of losing the illusion of institutional support. Knowing that it is an illusion does not make it easier. I have separated from my husband and have taken the extraordinary step of moving from academia into esthiology. I now attend the Aveda Institute in Washington, DC. By the time this book is published, I, and my class of "spa sisters"—who, by the way, represent the diversity and power I call for here—will be licensed estheticians.

Not much has changed culturally. Student loan debt and college costs continue to rise. Campus child care continues to be nonexistent. College continues to be a racial, gender, class, and disability contact zone, sometimes with devastating results (although sometimes with heartening ones). Even as college costs go up, for first-generation, poor, and Black students, a college degree can be life changing. Higher education still struggles with gender, racial, and disability differences. Mothers still, at least anecdotally, report feeling penalized, and higher ed still handles family leave badly, especially for contingent faculty. And for those of us raising children with high needs, caregiver burnout is real.

As I begin my second book, a monograph about disability and fandom, I constantly experience the consequences of giving up access to a university's repository of knowledge. I encounter delays, spend time searching for open access journals, and, at times, finally break down and pay for academic books. As I write my current book proposal, I find myself frustrated by the lack of access, which leads to slow progress. However, I have established a method for how I keep making the sausage. The first step is what all writing instructors will tell you, but it remains true: write about what you care about. As an independent scholar, you will do so much digging, tweeting, pleading, and beating your digital head into paywalls that, if you lack a real, rooted passion for the project, you'll burn out quickly. I find that my discipline and its networks are more amenable to independent scholars than others. Popular culture and fan studies tend to be more open to those of us on the outside and are more likely to help with access to sources and other materials. Connect with scholars online, particularly via Twitter and Facebook groups, where questions like "Does anyone know the history of trigger warnings?" get answered. This is a real-life example of a question I answered, providing citations from Alexis Lothian's work. Her work influenced me to make conference presentations accessible to d/Deaf and hard of hearing audience members via online scripts. Meredith Guthrie, the chair of the Mid-Atlantic Popular and American Culture Association conference where I first did this, tweeted it out, thus calling further attention to the practice.

I would also suggest that independent scholars resist the urge to write entire books at once. By this, I do not mean that monographs are out of reach of the independent scholar, but instead that chapter by chapter is the best way to proceed. Carefully considered scope, methodology, and arguments help, but research partnerships do as well. Snags will include human research that would require institutional review board (IRB) approval, as well as the challenges of revising and copyediting while balancing the needs of the rest of your life.

I do not feel what other scholars may feel when they leave academia, what Pryal calls a kind of identity loss, because my formal training was only two years and because now I control that identity far more than I ever did before.[15] I am not at the mercy of teaching schedules or commutes, and I do not follow the whims of irritable bosses. I sit down and write and research—and, yes, accrue overdue fines. The identity of "scholar" belongs to me much more than ever before. My research feeds my poetry and vice versa. I work my way toward Pryal's middle lane—the one where my mental health and my family's well-being hold equal place with my productivity, my new life, my education, and my work. And no matter how much labor it takes to make the system of my home and writing run, it no longer goes unnoticed: my children are happier, my son's therapist tells me I'm doing great, and my colleagues both in academia and in the beauty world support me.

Collegial support shows up in many forms. Former teaching buddy Joseph Fruscione and I now write and job search together. Former GW colleague Katherine Larsen is my series editor at the University of Iowa Press. Each poem that is published is met with a chorus of support from my professorial, poetry, and other friends. And as I go back to school with women aged twenty-two to mid-forties, my nickname in the classroom, "Mama Kat," indicates that I'm viewed as someone who has their backs and who will listen to their knowledge and expertise.

The economic, family, and gender concerns faced by most women in higher ed, as well as the desire for creative freedom, informed my decision to become an independent scholar. Having support from an institution can be important, but institutions exist to perpetuate themselves and what they value. Increasingly, they do not value the time, effort, and creative thinking of someone like me, who has obligations outside the institution, lacks the credentials to fit a financial bracket, and does not necessarily provide the institution with clout or status. We're too unruly. But, as Baker suggests, unruliness works in our favor: "Unruliness can be the path to liberation, to being who you are, to claiming the space to exist on your own terms."[16] People like me, who produce in multiple genres, who work in unorthodox ways, who raise unusual children, and who get things done, come hell or high water, are not always welcome or comfortable in rigid institutions. Let the institutions burn. We're better suited carving our own paths, in the middle lane.

NOTES

Disclaimer: The contents of this chapter reflect the views of the chapter author alone, and not those of the volume editors or press.

1. Kelly J. Baker, "Pursuing Happiness for All Women," *Women in Higher Education*, June 7, 2018, https://www.wihe.com/article-details/72 /pursuing-happiness-for-all-women/?ix=20.

2. Ruth Hammond, "Editor's Note: Hope and Worry by the Numbers," *Almanac of Higher Education*, August 20, 2018, https://www.chronicle .com/article/HopeWorry-by-the-Numbers/244154?cid=cp214.

3. Kelly J. Baker, "Necessary Unruliness," *Women in Higher Education*, August 31, 2017, https://www.wihe.com/article-details/46/necessary-un ruliness/?ix=40.

4. Hammond, "Editor's Note."

5. Baker, "Pursuing Happiness."

6. Katie Rose Guest Pryal, "Quit Lit Is about Labor Conditions," *Women in Higher Education*, June 7, 2018, https://www.wihe.com/article -details/74/quit-lit-is-about-labor-conditions/?ix=20.

7. Sebastian Kyle Vitale, "The Joy of Kids for Teacher-Scholar," *Inside Higher Ed*, January 9, 2019, https://www.insidehighered.com /advice/2019/01/09/benefits-academic-work-having-children-opinion;

Hammond, "Editor's Note"; Katie Rose Guest Pryal, "Find the Middle Lane," *Women In Higher Education*, October 3, 2018, https://www.wihe .com/article-details/84/find-the-middle-lane/.

8. Pryal, "Find the Middle Lane."

9. Pryal, "Quit Lit Is about Labor Conditions."

10. Hammond, "Editor's Note."

11. Digest of Education Statistics, 2015 (NCES 2016-014), table 311.10, chart (US Department of Education, National Center for Education Statistics, 2016), https://nces.ed.gov/fastfacts/display.asp?id=60; Joseph Grigely, "The Neglect Demographic: Faculty Members with Disabilities," *Chronicle of Higher Education*, June 27, 2017, https://nces.ed.gov/fastfacts /display.asp?id=60.

12. Pryal, "Find the Middle Lane."

13. Baker, "Necessary Unruliness."

14. Baker, "Necessary Unruliness."

15. Pryal, "Quit Lit Is about Labor Conditions."

16. Baker, "Necessary Unruliness."

9

Being a Full-Time Parent and a Part-Time Scholar

VALERIE SCHUTTE

On June 20, 2014, I successfully defended my dissertation in history on books dedicated to Queen Mary I of England in front of my five-person committee at the University of Akron. I was exactly twenty weeks pregnant. I graduated in August 2014 and gave birth to a son that October. I had planned on taking a semester or year off to be at home with my newborn before pursuing an academic job. Because my husband's business is location-bound, my career goal was never really a tenure-track teaching position that required moving, although that would have been nice, but a local part-time or adjunct position so that I only would work and arrange child care (courtesy of my wonderful mother) for two days a week. I even looked into academic journal editorial jobs that I could do from home.

However, all that changed the day I had my son and he had to be taken to our nearest children's hospital because of a life-threatening medical condition. Over the course of the seventy-five days he spent there, undergoing numerous surgeries and procedures, I decided that I would no longer pursue a teaching career at all and instead would be a full-time stay-at-home mom, devoted to my son's health care. I have never looked back on that decision, and would like to share below how in the intervening five years I have balanced being a stay-at-home mom to a child with medical needs and being a nontraditional scholar.

About one month before I had my son, I had submitted a revised version of my dissertation for publication in Palgrave Macmillan's Queenship and Power series, after having a chance meeting with the series coeditor, Carole Levin, that year at the International Medieval Congress at Kalamazoo. At a lunch off campus I told her about my dissertation project on Queen Mary I and her books, and she immediately supported it and wanted it for her series. Having already submitted my final draft to my committee prior to my defense, I went about amending my dissertation, making it more suitable for publication. It was that lunch that stimulated my nontraditional academic career, and Carole has been one of its greatest supporters.

In December 2014, while my son was still in the hospital, I received an email from the history editor at Palgrave Macmillan informing me that my book had been accepted for publication. I had actually forgotten that I had submitted the book proposal in the first place. My son came home for good on Christmas Eve that year, and while he remained my focus, my family encouraged me to prepare my manuscript and go through with its publication, even though it was no longer as important to me. It was during that process that I realized that, even if teaching was no longer in my future, I had pursued a history degree because I loved history and doing research. I could still do research from home, and beneficially (although it has taken some hindsight to see it), it served as a positive distraction from the seemingly never-ending doctors' appointments and two-to-three-times-a-week in-home therapies that my son endured. I submitted my final manuscript on January 31, 2015.

I attended one academic conference in 2015 because, as with my book, I had applied to it while I was pregnant and unaware of my son's condition. I had actually applied and been accepted into more, but decided to back out of them. The one conference I did attend was the Early Book Society meeting in Oxford in July, and while I was incredibly hesitant to go, again, my family supported my research and academic career. Also, I had barely left the house in six months besides going to doctors' appointments, so I think they wanted me to do something for myself. The conference was the best thing I could have done for myself at that time. I was able to socialize, discuss my work, and stay active within the scholarly community. I presented a paper on books dedicated to Henry VII, and that essay was later published in the *Journal of the Early Book Society*.

Since then, I have continued to actively present and publish my work. After 2015, my son's health stabilized and I felt more comfortable leaving him with family members so that I could do research trips and go to conferences. In 2016, I attended several conferences, two of which were in London, and gave my first invited lecture on books related to Queens Mary and Elizabeth Tudor at Christ Church Canterbury University that November. Currently, I attend about four conferences a year, one of which is usually in the United Kingdom, so that I can be with other scholars and network.

Conferences have truly been the key to my career as an independent scholar. With no departmental colleagues that I see regularly, I rely on conferences for many things. They are something I look forward to as a break from being home so much (although I miss my son dreadfully when I go). I use them to network, and now, to visit friends I have made from attending the same conferences regularly. I find that conferences also stimulate my own research as I come home energized with new ideas on how to approach my own research or with thoughtful feedback on a paper that I delivered. Nothing makes me happier than when I get a comment about someone enjoying my paper or having read my work, knowing that I have engaged in nothing but self-promotion and hard work. It validates that my nontraditional career is worth it and reassures me that I have made the right decision to be an independent scholar and stay-at-home mom.

As mentioned above, when my son was first born, I had decided to give up on an academic career altogether, and would have done so if my family had not been so supportive. Once I got into the research again and the excitement of publishing my first book, I realized that in a way I needed to keep working on my research to feel complete. My husband and son make me have a complete family, but I really needed something for myself, where I felt accomplished. Reading and writing also gave me a release from the initial stress of not understanding my son's condition and all of the hardships that would come with it. History is familiar and comforting to me, and I always get relaxed and happy when I have a good work day or learn or discover something new. I become a better mother when I feel like I am contributing both at home and with my work. It makes me feel good about myself.

I have never really felt any guilt for choosing to be a part-time scholar, except for when I sometimes go on research trips or to conferences and am away for a few days or a week (the limit I have set for myself for time away). Truthfully, I do not feel guilty for leaving my son, because I know it benefits us both to not spend every moment together, but I feel guilty when he stays at my mother's house for a week as I do not want him to be an inconvenience for her. However, I think my mother and stepfather enjoy the time with him as much as I enjoy the time in a library or giving a paper.

I have really been able to complete so many research projects in the last five years because child care has not been an issue. I have a very large family and we all live in close proximity, so there are plenty of people who offer to watch my son regularly. Most helpful have been my grandmother and my mother and stepfather. My grandmother frequently comes over to spend a couple of hours with my son, during which I sit in my office and type up notes, write emails, or wrap up loose ends for projects. I do not get much research done during those visits because my son is often playing in the next room and making a good bit of noise, or popping in the office to say "hi" and see what I am working on.

My mother now watches my son one day per week at her house, and it is on that day that I get the majority of my work done each week. Often those visits turn into sleepovers, and my husband and I have been able to go on some date nights as a result too. My mother and stepfather also take my son every time I go away for research, which has been instrumental in assisting me to pursue my part-time academic career.

When my son was napping for multiple hours a day, I was able to work for about one hour every day. But now that he is a toddler and naps are inconsistent, I do not get much work done in a week outside of the day he is with my mother, unless he gets sufficiently distracted with a toy or television show. What this has done for me, is cause me to become hyperorganized (I have always been an organized person) and plan out what I would like to get done ahead of time so as to maximize my time and progress. I keep a detailed list of projects I am working on, their due dates, and the order in which I need to work on them to make sure that everything gets done on time. I now work smarter and faster, knowing that I may not be able to get back to an article or a source for at least a week.

Besides attending conferences and publishing my first monograph, I have published numerous book chapters and journal articles, as well as edited or coedited four collections of essays. Being involved in edited collections has proven immensely helpful to my career as well. Each has had its own set of challenges, but each has also honed my skills as an editor and allowed me to work with a wide range of scholars, with whom I never would have come into contact otherwise. Through these collections, I have proven myself to be timely, able to multitask, and thoughtful with feedback. These books have opened doors for me and helped to establish my scholarly reputation, not only because my name is on the cover but also because I have published on a wide range of subjects.

I have also recently begun to volunteer for service in scholarly organizations as another way to stay involved with fellow scholars even as I work from home. In many cases I am simply organizing panels for various conferences, which allows me to keep email contacts with interested panelists and with conference organizers who know that I am willing and able to chair and organize sessions. Recently I applied to be on various executive committees for conferences, knowing that being on the board of an academic organization will solidify my reputation as an independent scholar.

Since 2014, I have made a conscious decision and effort to be an independent scholar whose first priority is being a mother. This career path has worked for me, and I have never looked back at what could have been. I also have no desire to return to a traditional academic teaching job, for I have realized that my true passion is research and writing and that is what I am best at doing.

However, this path has not been without its pitfalls and challenges. To a large extent, I have felt rather alone as an independent scholar. I have found that there is a real lack of scholarly support and community. I do not have an academic department of colleagues with whom I can have lunch and chat about my research projects or who will read drafts of book chapters or essays. Rather, I try to network as much as possible at conferences so that I can resort to email conversations about my research and where it is headed or ask a friend to read drafts.

I thought I might have kept that community at the University of Akron, but that was quickly gone once I left. I entered the graduate program there in the fall of 2010, completed my coursework in two years, and wrote my dissertation in about one and a half years; my committee revisions and defense took my final spring and summer semesters. Since leaving the program, I have only really communicated with former professors and advisors if I happen to see one of them at a conference. There was no effort on their part to help me with job applications, interviews, or even advice on publishing my dissertation. All of that I picked up myself while attending conferences and speaking with people about my research and my situation.

I do not harbor ill feelings toward the department, yet I, as I believe many other graduates do, felt grossly unprepared for what came after earning a PhD. The job market has been poor for a while for those of us specializing in early modern Britain who reside in the United States, and that I was warned about. Yet the only offer of assistance that I received was when I was told I could get on the adjunct teaching rotation at Akron until another job came along. I passed on the opportunity firstly because of my son, but also because I had been commuting an hour and a half each way to the university and could not justify continuing to do so just to teach a class or two, especially if they were early morning or in the evening. Perhaps I would have had better support if I had stayed as an adjunct because I would have seen my former professors regularly and could have asked for advice or even letters of recommendation. But as soon as I made the decision not to teach, that opportunity for connection was gone.

When I was at Akron, I was a teaching assistant for two years and an editorial assistant for *Civil War History*, because the editor-in-chief was a professor in the department. That year as an editorial assistant was invaluable to my being an independent scholar; I learned about publishing and how to work with an academic press. As the editorial assistant, I updated the website, kept a record of all submissions and their stages in the review process, sent emails to contributors about permissions, and read over copy edits and proofs. I still do all of those things regularly and because of that experience I have been able to edit four collections so far with minimal surprises (except how difficult it is to get people to turn things in on time).

My two years as a teaching assistant I have found much less valuable and impactful on my current career path. Obviously, I have given up teaching; I learned as a TA that I never really enjoyed teaching in the first place. I chose to get a PhD in history because I liked to research history, not because I wanted to stand in front of a classroom of glassy-eyed freshmen and describe *The Iliad* and gender to them (my experience, courtesy of teaching one year of Humanities in the Western Tradition, the only TA position remotely related to European history majors). Yet, even when I was considering pursuing a teaching position, I often felt underprepared as a TA because I was not taught any methods or given any instructions. I entered my first semester of my PhD knowing that I had one section of discussion for Humanities in the Western Tradition and had to write my own syllabus, lead weekly discussions, and write my own assignments, grading scale, and quizzes. My lack of confidence in my abilities as a TA then translated into a decreasing desire to pursue teaching full-time.

Along with lack of scholarly support from a department, I have also suffered from not being taken seriously as a scholar because I am not in a tenure-track position at a university or actively pursuing one. I know that I have been excluded from projects because I was not thought of as academically valuable. I have even been told by my former mentors that if I don't pursue teaching I will have wasted all of my academic training, as though teaching at the university level is all I am qualified to do with a PhD in history. And while I continue to be underestimated, I have determined that there is no one correct path or career for a scholar.

This has caused me to become more confident in myself and my research. I know that not everyone finds my research interesting, and I have been rejected from journals because many people think my work is too literary to be history, but not literary enough to be English. However, rejection is part of every academic job. No authors publish every piece they write, and sometimes journal reviewers are cranky. But I have gained confidence and know that even if something gets rejected by a journal, I can always try to publish it elsewhere or repurpose it, for instance, as a book chapter. For example, I recently cowrote a book chapter with a colleague, only to have the peer reviewer suggest that my portion be removed so as to have more room for my colleague to expound upon her work. Since then, I repurposed my portion of the chapter and had it accepted into another edited collection. I have also become bolder about approaching other scholars with whom I would like to work and making myself invaluable to projects in which I would like to participate. If I see a conference I would like to attend but am unable to because of timing or expense, I often email the conference organizers with what I would have presented to see if they are interested, in the event that a conference proceedings is published, a tactic that has worked in my favor. Because I have not been taken seriously, I have made an effort to attend academic conferences and publish as much as possible in order to establish a name and reputation for myself as an expert on early modern queens and their books.

I would like to see the stigma of being an independent scholar removed. Too often, when I tell people at conferences that I am independent and a stay-at-home mom, I can immediately read disapproval on their faces. They suggest I am not taking academia seriously and frequently ask when I will look for jobs again or what problem kept me from finding one in the first place. I have resigned myself to these questions now, but at first I wanted to scream every time someone suggested that my work is not worthwhile because I have chosen not to do it full-time. However, I would be willing to guess that contrary to many of these traditional scholars, I can work on my research whenever I want, in whatever manner I want; and I only have to push it off for family reasons, not because I am overloaded from teaching. I feel, in a sense, freer and happier than when I was at a university all day and then came home to read and write all night.

Beyond not being taken seriously, there are also practical downsides to being an independent scholar. Lack of funding for travel expenses has also proven quite challenging. Independent scholars do qualify for some bursaries and grants, and this pool of funding actually seems to have been growing in the last couple of years. More early career researchers are having difficulty finding full-time work, and academic organizations have been making travel funds specifically available for those who have received a PhD within the past five years and who are not employed. This excludes me and, as a result, I have borne all costs of my research and conference attendance personally. For many, this would be an obstacle too substantial to overcome.

But, definitely, the most challenging aspect of being a part-time, independent scholar is limited access to sources. I do not live in an area with early modern English history archives, and, with no university affiliation and credentials, I can access only minimal online databases for the sources that I need and would love to have. That is partially why I chose to study books related to Tudor kings and queens, because I knew I would never be able to undertake research that required long-term archival visits. I cannot rent books from a university library; although I could visit a university library and use a book in their collection on-site, I cannot request a book from another library. So I often turn to Amazon and hope that I can buy a used copy of a book instead. I also cannot access the majority of academic databases. I have found ways around getting on the most common databases, such as JSTOR, and friends have often lent me their own credentials if I really need immediate access to something. I try not to ask for this often, and will never divulge who helps me because I do not want anyone to get in trouble for sharing their university password with me. In a few instances, I have even pleaded with friends to get something for me via interlibrary loan, which is a resource I greatly miss.

Based on my experiences, I think there are many ways that universities, archives, and societies could better support independent scholars. Often, it seems that monetary support would be the most useful, and in many ways, it would be invaluable to independent scholars. Yet, my biggest need is not money (as independent scholars may simply be working a different job and societies are starting to recognize that early career researchers are in a similar financial position to postgraduates), but the recognition that I, too, am a contributing member of academic society, even though I do not have a university affiliation.

It is not terribly hard to get a university affiliation if you are an independent scholar. The easiest way is to simply affiliate yourself with the institution that granted your PhD. You can still claim them as your home school, without getting any support from them in return. A surprising number of universities also offer honorary fellowships, a simple process that is usually handled within a few emails, and the institutions can then claim connections with scholars across the globe. Again, these honorary sorts of positions often offer no real benefit, other than being able to use their name as your affiliation.

However, I have chosen not to affiliate myself with a university, without having an active role at that university. I am proud that I work from home, largely on my own, and that I have achieved as much as I have. Yet, I know that I do not get asked to give guest lectures because I am not affiliated with a university. I am not a "prestigious" scholar to be called upon to give lectures or even interviews when a new movie related to queenship or early modern English history comes out.

My biggest suggestion to help independent scholars would be for university libraries and online databases to offer single-person options for access to sources. For instance, I am always writing about various Tudor queens. Having access to State Papers Online would be invaluable as I cannot regularly get to the National Archives at Kew. Yet I have reached out to this database, via email and by actually speaking with a representative at a conference, and they have no intention of having a personal subscription option, only an institutional subscription option. If databases such as this one had a personal option, I would happily pay a small fee to have access to the things I need without having to bother friends to "just check" something for me. Interlibrary loan should offer something similar. If I had access to that service, it could save me from having to buy books in order to read just a few pages of one chapter. Additionally, it is not as though all traditional scholars have access to these services, and I am sure some of them, particularly at small institutions that only subscribe to minimal archiving services, would be happy to have a personal option as well.

The online publication of primary sources will continue to make my career as an independent scholar easier. There is hot debate at conferences over whether researchers should use sources photocopied for databases or sit in the archives where they can touch the contemporary materials. Not everyone has the opportunity or ability to sit in the archives for long periods of time. When sources are available online, scholars such as myself can read them even if they cannot touch and smell the paper. These sources are simply invaluable to nontraditional scholars and, I imagine, to traditional scholars and graduate students as well. Universities do not have limitless budgets to spend on research trips, and digitization allows scholars to have output while keeping costs down.

Overall though, as I mentioned earlier, I have no regrets. The benefits of my situation are excellent: I spend every day with my son, focus on my own publications, and only work on projects that I find meaningful because I do not have to work toward tenure. For now, I see myself continuing on this path as an independent researcher indefinitely. This is for many reasons. First, and foremost, I have decided to put my family first. Even as my toddler son enters school, I would like to experience that process with him. He will be attending a private school, and I plan to volunteer my time and skills to his school and to any potential therapies and medical treatments he will need in the future.

Second, as also mentioned earlier, I have no desire to teach, either full-time or part-time. I know I do not want to enter a classroom regularly if I am not teaching about my own research or subjects in which I am truly interested (I am looking at you, humanities). I have friends who live to teach their students as much as possible, yet I do not feel that same reward after leading a good discussion. However, I love to talk about history and research, and would love to have more opportunities to guest lecture in traditional classrooms, in online history courses, and at departmental or societal meetings. These are the types of activities that I find rewarding and worthwhile. Being invited to give a talk would validate that my activities at home do not go unnoticed.

Third, I simply like being in control of my own career. I can choose to work on projects that interest me with no pressure to write a certain number of articles or books or else fear losing my job or funding. I can choose to sit at my computer in lounge clothes, drinking a whole pot of tea, or to just not do anything academic for a week or two, with no repercussions, except that I feel lazy.

One final piece of advice that I would like to share for those who are part-time scholars or are considering being independent, but would still like to be taken seriously, is to never say "no." I almost never turn down a book review, a project, or an essay that someone asks me to be a part of or to write. I know that if I turn down enough things, people will eventually stop asking. This strategy has opened several doors for me; it seems that as I participate in more projects and publish more, this cements my position as a serious academic on a nontraditional path. Once I have reached a plateau where I feel comfortable in my career and reputation, I will become more selective in what I do.

I never expected that, five years after earning my PhD in history, I would be as accomplished as I am. But, here I am, having just signed contracts for my second and third monographs, with plans for a fourth already typed up, and they will wait for me to write one book at a time. Being a part-time scholar and full-time mother has been more rewarding than I could have ever imagined when I decided to pursue a doctorate in the first place. There are so many options for part-time scholars, but having a child and working at my own pace is the one that has worked best for me.

PART FOUR

FROM THE UNIVERSITY
TO FREEDOM

10

Freeing the PhD—Solving an Identity Crisis

VAY CAO

No one wants to fail.

Yet from the moment I started my first day as a graduate student in 2007, I was all but destined to fail.

This is because, like so many others, I believed that getting a PhD means that success is defined solely by "making it" to the next step in the academic food chain. This belief was supported by the data points I had been exposed to thus far.

My father became a tenured professor after immigrating to the United States, finishing his PhD in four years, postdoc in two, then making his way steadily along the tenure track.

A renowned professor in whose lab I did undergraduate research ruled an entire university building floor filled with dedicated and productive postdoctoral research fellows.

A postdoc I worked with from that lab received a faculty position soon after I graduated.

The path to success was clear. Get the PhD. Publish an amazing paper. Get a faculty position. Win at life.

Everything made sense.

But looking back from a wholly different vantage point after over five years working in a start-up company, launching an alternative career course and professional advocacy platform for researchers called Free the PhD, and following the different life journeys of fellow academics through coaching and workshops, I see what the glaring flaw was in my career analysis methodology back then.

Simply put, the scale bar on my worldview was waaaaaay off. Like, orders of magnitude off.

At the time, I had been looking at just a tiny part of society that was open and available for consideration. On top of that, all my life advice and vicarious experiences had come exclusively from an academic demographic—talk about biased datasets!

All the evidence in the research world and beyond over the last few decades point to one inevitability: that the majority of PhD holders will not be employed in academic research positions. We either accept this fact and adjust our career-related hypotheses and activities, or pay the heavily stressful price of exceptionalism as generations of PhDs did and unfortunately continue to do.

It should not need repeating that there are simply not enough permanent academic positions for every PhD that is produced in the multitude of research groups across all fields and institutions around the world every year. More importantly, academic research—like any worthy endeavor—benefits from a great diversity of participants from varied backgrounds, personalities, and skill sets.

It's unrealistic to assume that such diverse participants will all want, or be able, to stay within any singular employment scenario for a lifetime.

In light of these facts, it's time to stop basing our collective PhD identities and definitions of success on baselines of the past.

Instead, let's free ourselves to examine exactly what it is that we can extract from the PhD experience, and how we can combine this with our unique attributes and perspectives to impact society the best way we can.

So . . . how exactly do we go about doing this?

Identify What You Love in Research and in Life

I don't know about you, but I haphazardly embarked on my PhD journey without a clear future purpose for the degree. You could say I didn't have a better idea of what to do after college, so I "fell" into the PhD track as the next logical step in obtaining a higher education.

Naturally, going with the flow isn't always the best reason to do a PhD. In fact, it's a pretty weak reason to dedicate the next four to six years of your life to any venture! Yet I didn't feel there were other options at the time. I identified with being a scientist, and was so used to the progression and structure of academia that it seemed a safer bet than striking out on the job market.

This feeling was compounded by the fact that I didn't like the day-to-day pipetting and small-scale work available to an undergraduate microbiology major. I realized my personal interests were far more tied to cognitive- and behavioral-level questions, so I made my first big career pivot into neuroscience for my PhD.

Thank goodness for this decision. Since I fell in love with the subject matter, my personal interests not only helped me through the ups and downs of the PhD experience but also guided my career trajectory into the commercial side of a neurotechnology company after I left academia.

The beginning of graduate school was filled with energy and the magic of novelty. There were amazingly interesting scientific questions to ask: about how the brain changed during learning and how groups of cells worked together to support important brain functions and behavior. I had amazing resources to address those questions, and interesting ideas about what we might find.

But vague possibilities and shiny new toys get old quickly if you discover that your inner fire isn't actually ignited by academic experimentation itself, or by reading literature and writing grants for months or years at a time.

I started getting depressed in my third year—it's hard not to when nothing seems to work day in and day out! This is when I began to—unwittingly—lay the vital foundations for my future career. When opportunities came my way to work on side projects, I took them. Actively seeking out opportunities to try new things, I answered classified ads for writing and art gigs on Craigslist and attended local Meetup groups. The motivation was primarily to distract myself from the constant failures plaguing my research project at the time, but along the way I picked up invaluable skill sets and made new friends who helped to keep me energized in my academic life.

By the end of the PhD, I had a completed doctoral thesis and a thorough understanding of my research field. I had also racked up a portfolio of written articles, along with years of video editing, illustration, and master of ceremonies experience. I tutored occasionally on weekends, joined an a cappella group on campus, and served on our graduate student council.

These projects outside of academia were good for my mental and social health. This fact in and of itself should be reason enough to reserve time for things you enjoy. Straddling the intersectional identities of scientist, communicator, community builder, and creative was true to who I was, so it made me happy. Later, I also realized that the combination of one or more traditional identities is in fact an effective and impactful way to demonstrate your value as a unique and versatile individual.

Not taking time to indulge your personal interests beyond

academia is the number one résumé killer for every PhD I've career coached through Free the PhD. Individuals looking for a bench research job might be ok if their research skills fall into sectors where commercial, nonprofit, or government employers already recognize their value.

But for those PhDs whose research skills don't neatly fall into a ready-made job description, or PhDs who want to pivot into a new career path, the road is much harder. People fear what they don't understand, and many PhDs are ignored by recruiters and hiring managers for this very reason—we don't make any sense to them!

To combat this, you need to become much more strategic in the use of your time. You must apply the scientific method to yourself, and modify your career hypotheses and job application experiments based on the data you collect from the results of your job hunt.

So what's the protocol for this?

The first, most important, and often-skipped step of building and maintaining a healthy, agile, employable PhD identity is figuring out exactly what it is that makes you tick.

Not what you think your PhD demands. Not what your principal investigator (PI) or parents think. Not what society wants you to do.

Do you know what drives you? Because if you don't even know what you want or are good at, how will you convince an employer to hire you for it?

Do you love digging through spreadsheets? Keeping lab records in order? Designing experiments?

How about mentoring high school students? Setting up collaborations? Presenting posters and talks?

And just as importantly, do you know what you don't like? Have you tried enough things hands-on that you can honestly say how you feel from personal experience?

Preferences and passions are different for every person, driven by each individual's unique combination of past experiences, personality, and life circumstances. For your long-term health and happiness, these drives should not be ignored.

For me, I loved uncovering new trends and observing my research subjects. But these weren't the only things I loved.

I loved science communication; driving outreach to diverse groups; building community and coaching others. I had a knack for creative expression and the arts. And to my surprise, I found that the things that ignite my fire could be found and pursued effectively in the wide world outside academia, particularly in the start-up community.

At the tail end of my PhD, I landed an application scientist position in a young company that valued these things I loved, alongside my research background.

This job offer was no coincidence. I started sending job applications into the void in my third year as I was pursuing my research and hobbies. I got no bites until this job came along. This time, unlike most of the other jobs I barely understood, it was crystal clear that we were a perfect fit for each other, and I made sure to reflect our unique match in my cover letter and résumé.

No one gets any job by accident—or even pure luck. I didn't come into this job application with zero years of relevant experience, as many fellow PhDs unfortunately attempt to do. Instead, I had five years of technically relevant experience (the PhD research experience gave me microscopy, animal behavior, and experimental skills they valued) and more than three years of business-relevant writing, freelancing, and leadership experience (from those hobbies and volunteering). This made me stand out against job candidates who had concentrated purely on academic science for five or even ten or more years.

As we'll discuss later, technical skills only get us so far in life.

If you want to make your professional life easier while you are in graduate school, diversify, diversify, diversify your time. Identify jobs that interest you in your first one to two years. Spend the rest of your time getting involved in side activities that are relevant to that career path. Get to know people outside your research sphere who can help you get where you want to go one to two years before you want to leave.

It is never too early for this. Never.

Sometimes it's hard to hear, but there is no magic industry training program, paid certificate, or secret formula that will guarantee us a job outside academia. Our luckiness is accumulated and built over time, and only comes to you if you are willing to take the needed actions to attract it.

And so, after I got the final job offer, I took a leap of faith, committed to leaving everything I knew, and signed the contract.

A New Identity: Life and Lessons from a Start-Up

The biomedical and technology-related world outside academia is actually not all that different from life within it and yet, it simultaneously seems light years away—a speedier, rawer, and for me, far more exhilarating ride.

I left the familiarity of the lab to join a small, actively growing start-up on the other side of the country. The company was a spin-off from an academic lab, featuring a product originally developed by PhDs. The company was cofounded by their PI. The hiring manager I interviewed with was a PhD. Our customers were PhDs. You get the picture.

It's rare to exit academia and enter such an academia-adjacent business. Compared to fellow PhDs who leave to join Fortune 500s or industries serving traditional customers in banking or management consulting, my culture shock was not even that extreme.

Yet the spirit and needs of a young start-up overrode all shadows of similarity between my previous academic identity and my developing professional one. I joined a team of two serving a hundred customer sites around the world. I initially spent half my time in the company lab developing experimental applications similar to what I used in my PhD work, and half the time interacting with customers.

Immediately, the biggest thing that stood out as a start-up employee versus an academic researcher was the juxtaposition of a frantic pace of projects, coupled with utter ambiguity. A lifetime up to then of academic rules and traditions left me expecting workplace guidance and baselines with which to measure my work.

You get none of that in a young start-up.

At first, this was distressing. What information should be included in the product package for customers? When should revisions to this web page be done by? What are the protocols for answering an email to an angry customer?

As new projects arose and new challenges appeared, I figured things out. This process can be summed up as doing your homework, asking the right people, communicating needs efficiently, and advocating effectively for resources.

Also—just trying it out and dealing with the results.

Becoming more mature as a professional with these so-called soft skills allowed me to work on a multitude of cross-departmental projects with real-world, potentially immediate impacts on customers and colleagues alike.

Just like in science itself, you don't always have the right answer. Sometimes no one does. In the face of ambiguity, you just have to run some experiments, look at the data, and then communicate a decision, even with incomplete information, as terrifying as that might be.

As a result, my love for discovery and desire for intellectual engagement have yet to stand idle. I still apply the scientific method all the time!

Combining scientific expertise with sharpened social and relationship-building skills in a business context set a foundation for me to migrate through the company, growing with it as it grew over the next few years. I finished out my first year working in the lab and one-on-one with customers, then branched out to tackle marketing, training, and outreach projects. I had the opportunity to travel across the United States and Asia, giving departmental seminars at many universities, attending the same conferences I did as a student (only now I was the one giving out free stuff), and teaching customers in their labs and at our office.

Recently, an opportunity to move horizontally to the sales department arose, so I now find myself responsible for managing the commercial growth of the Asia Pacific region for my company. Once again, this is a completely new role with new challenges and pressures, but draws upon a growing professional foundation built over the last few years.

This type of role was not even on my radar when I was in graduate school, but when an opportunity to develop new, transferable skills comes your way, I've learned that it's wise to take it.

Once empowered with the building blocks of a career, many doors are available for PhD-trained individuals to open if they so choose.

Just like in graduate school, catalyzing change in your PhD identity outside academia takes time, effort, and purposeful action. The following three lessons were invaluable to my professional development, and have kept me excited about the future:

Drive your own career growth.

Learn to say no.

Never stop learning.

Let's see how these lessons can help you move your career forward both within and outside academia.

Drive Your Own Career Growth

The historical mentor–trainee relationship within most academic research institutions makes it difficult for many graduate students or even postdoctoral fellows to clearly define their professional goals independent of their PI's goals for the greater research group. This can lead to wonderful outcomes when the trainee's and PI's goals are mutually beneficial and amplified by open communication.

However, if circumstances are not ideal, the power imbalance between PhD candidate or postdoc versus the PI can lead to tragedy in various forms. I know PhD candidates and postdocs who found themselves rudely abandoned or kicked out of a lab with little warning when funding ran out; foreign postdocs who were held to more demanding work expectations than citizens because of visa vulnerabilities; students who tolerated toxic work environments despite disintegrating mental and physical health because they thought this was just the way things are.

In all relationships, whoever has the most leverage has more control. If you want to avoid or minimize the chances of unpleasant surprises, you must take the initiative to empower yourself with more than one exit option.

Academic trainees tend to automatically place their immediate career prospects in the hands of just one person—their PI—so choose this person and manage this relationship wisely. PhDs should be cognizant of what they want to achieve in graduate school or as a postdoc and should have open dialogue about this early on with the person that has the most influence on their ability to get what they want.

If you find yourself hesitant to push on this conversation with your primary mentor due to lack of support, this does not mean you should abandon what matters to you. It means you should seek a second or third opinion, and perhaps a second or third mentor inside or outside the lab. It helps to have supportive figures in your life who are open and available for advice, encouragement, and practically speaking, recommendation letters or references down the line. Your career is at least as important as a medical condition, so why would you not gather more data from multiple experts before you form important hypotheses?

The need to drive your own career is even more pronounced outside of academia. In most companies and social structures in general, you must learn how to ask for what you want. Titles, raises, promotions, exciting projects, and job offers do not fall out of the sky into your lap. No one can help you move forward—not even the most supportive mentor—if you don't communicate what you want.

Sometimes identifying your goals and putting them out there with your boss means being ok with not making everyone happy. It's not always pleasant to discuss plans with someone who does not share the same vision. It can be hard to give yourself permission to do this. However, developing professional maturity is learning how to negotiate competing desires and manage differing expectations. Managing in all directions (down to direct reports, across to colleagues, and up to bosses) is difficult, but worth practicing early and often.

In the start-up world, I have found it endlessly rewarding to consistently look for new ways to add value to a project, team, or department. In return, I earned opportunities to drive my own career. I saw a chance to use my writer's eye to edit our company website—I then got to work on conference materials and brochures and to revamp the company website and videos. I volunteered to travel on a seminar tour to a key customer region; that led to the chance to select and train a distribution partner for that region (which then led to other opportunities, etc.).

The unifying thread in all of this is that nothing new happens if you don't change your behavior. It all comes down to you deciding to take charge of your future, rather than letting your future happen to you. When you begin to take action, one small step at a time, you will be amazed at the butterfly effect you can create for your future self.

People outside academia routinely ask for what they want when it comes to job start dates, pay, titles, job responsibilities, resources, benefits, head-count (people to hire), flex time, internships, vacations, contract dates, timelines, and milestones. I watched, and I learned.

I gave myself permission to get out from the passenger's seat, and to slide in behind the wheel.

You can too.

Learn to Say No

One of the things we do not learn very well in a typical academic lab is time management. Although we can certainly talk about running multiple experiments in parallel, writing manuscripts while juggling analyses, learning new procedures, collecting time points, and managing research collaborators, we need to be aware of the context in which the term "time management" is usually used by employers. The number of competing priorities in an academic lab can pale in comparison to the workload, scale, and time sensitivity of many commercial, nonprofit, or large-scale government projects.

Not getting a project done by a certain date in academia might impact the pace of that person's project, or at worst, risk a big grant deadline or publication opportunity.

Then consider that in a government agency, being late on a deadline might impact fellow government workers across multiple departments, or perhaps hundreds of thousands of citizens in a municipality.

In a pharma company, missing timelines could mean the

difference between a drug candidate getting approved to start its arduous process toward reaching patients, or getting cut from the company's development pipeline.

In a start-up, meeting timelines can mean the difference between earning enough revenue to survive another year, to declaring bankruptcy and causing tens or hundreds of people to lose their jobs, in turn affecting all the members of their families.

Individual academic PhD or postdoc projects, by their inherent nature, tend to have more limited stakes and to impact primarily the lives of a few people directly involved in those projects (stakeholders, you can call them). Academic research projects also tend to have fuzzier and longer timelines. One to two years to complete a project is not uncommon, and some fields are known to routinely accumulate four to five years' worth of work before resulting in a publication or grant.

In contrast, some start-up companies run out of funding and shut down within six months, let alone five years. Outside of the academic world, when project timelines are often faster-paced and one person's actions can potentially impact many others, a sense of urgency and placing a high value on time is critical. Time is everyone's most nonrenewable resource, so the ability to say no to distractions becomes vital to survival and ultimate success.

All PhD scholars—both within and external to academia— would benefit from protecting their time and learning how to say no to tasks, projects, and even relationships that distract from what matters to you.

If you want to graduate in the next six months, you should think about whether the tantalizing new project your PI just threw your way is fruitful for that goal.

If you are interested in consulting jobs, you need to decide if scrolling through Instagram is a good use of your free time, as opposed to studying for case interviews.

If you're a second-year student and not sure what jobs are interesting to you, you must decide if your time is better spent reading another paper, or taking fifteen minutes from your day to cold email people on LinkedIn to ask for informational interviews. No one is immune to the impact of how they choose to spend their time. Start-up employees, management consultants, and yes, academic researchers will all experience impossible workloads and demands. No one can do it all—but everyone can prioritize, focus, and say no when necessary.

Just remember that when you say yes to everything others want, you may be actively deciding to say no to what you want. Own your time, or someone else will.

Never Stop Learning

Over the last year since I joined the business world, I have done more reading and active learning than I did in the last several years of my PhD. If I am honest with myself, I probably stopped learning from my research experience somewhere in my third year—when I was in the thick of conducting experiments and stressing out about whether or not things were working. I did not have time to learn new things, because I was so busy troubleshooting, collecting data, and tweaking protocols.

This learning plateau is a natural part of becoming an expert at something, and it's actually worth taking some pride in. When you stop learning, it means you have flailed, failed, and floundered through the painful process of moving from a novice to someone who knows what they're doing. You will now be much better at troubleshooting similar issues, and are hopefully also better at the process of learning itself, becoming more efficient and confident in your ability to figure new things out.

It is precisely this ability to learn that makes PhDs so valuable in any field they choose to pursue. Every field and endeavor requires learning, and as PhDs armed with the scientific method and the research process, we can be especially effective at pinning down addressable issues, gathering relevant data, and making quick progress in the face of the unknown.

In every new role at my company, I did new literature searches to broaden my knowledge and become more effective. This meant purchasing courses on time management and negotiation; books about training, marketing, customer service, and sales. I completed a free app-based MBA to obtain a basic business background, listened to podcasts about start-up life, and attended entrepreneurship conferences. I read about content strategy, negotiation, and management, and listened to friends and experts tell me about their experiences in the working world.

No matter what field you decide to move into, there is relevant knowledge, research, and wisdom to be gained that you don't have right now. We can never stop doing our homework if we want to stay relevant and employed.

Even for those who will remain in academia, continuing to learn new techniques, adopt new technologies, try new analyses, and use new ways to communicate your findings (#sciencetwitter) will be part of your road to success. PIs must describe in grants how their proposed project will advance the field—not maintain the status quo. New faculty members must demonstrate how they bring something new and different to the department they want to join. Departments must innovate to attract the best faculty and students. Research fields must evolve to keep up with new discoveries and regional economic pressures. Everyone must keep their eye on the horizon even as they concentrate on keeping their immediate footing. The field you are in is always creeping forward in multiple directions, and if you're not careful, will slide away and leave you behind.

Today, I still engage in nonstop reading, research, and informational interviewing despite having a job I love. I have made it a regular habit to network with strangers; I talk to more people at conferences than I ever did in graduate school and have accumulated a bookshelf (physical and digital) of resources with which to educate myself on the latest project I'm working on.

Why?

Because no one knows what the future holds, and nonstop learning is how we stay lucky.

Am I Still a Scientist? Defining What It Means to Be an Independent Scholar

Perhaps the biggest hurdle about leaving academia (besides the whole stressful process of actually getting a job offer) is the hardest to overcome, as it is purely psychological.

I stressed out for weeks over the idea that I would no longer be an academic once I took the job and left my postdoc. The ego can't help but protest when the benefits of a decision are unclear, and a valuable identity seems to be taken away.

Am I really giving up this hard-won social status and world I know so well?

Am I still smart and accomplished after I leave behind my academic trappings and laurels?

Am I a "real" PhD if my job isn't research focused or has nothing to do with my field?

Can I still make scholarly contributions to a field I love?

To be frank, it can be difficult to remain entrenched in original research activities after you leave certain fields. You may not be able to contribute in exactly the same way as before. As I stepped away from the bench, I would lose access to the fancy equipment, animal facilities, expensive reagents, and institutional credentials assumed necessary to add new knowledge to my field.

The reason for this lack of postacademic support for independent scholarship (especially in wet lab fields) is partly due to financial impracticalities. It may also be due to the fact that demand for it might not have been particularly great up until now.

So once again, as the realities change for all of us in and outside academia, it's up to us to redraw the boundaries around what we consider scholarly activities, and perhaps to catalyze new ways to provide more opportunities for people outside academia to stay involved.

Besides, what's a scholar anyway?

The Cambridge Dictionary defines the term "scholar" as "a person who studies a subject in great detail, especially at a university."

In American English, scholar means "a person with great knowledge, usually of a particular subject."[1]

Nowhere does the idea of a scholar absolutely require that a person must be conducting active research as a professor or principal investigator as defined by tenured academic standards. Think tanks, companies, nonprofits, media outlets, government agencies, and grassroots community organizations are all legitimate and active sources of scholarship.

You and I can continue to be active scholars at any time, if we choose to.

As an example, I published a review article and two original methods papers with my academic colleagues after I left my postdoc. Even as I moved away from the company lab and its bench-based publication potential, I found ways to contribute to two books being published by academic presses. I have now given seminars to hundreds of professors and students across the world, in top institutions and departments in my field—far more than I ever did as a "real" academic.

Many PhD peers and colleagues outside academia think more deeply about research and scholarly topics than they ever did before, because now they are informed by new perspectives, charged with undertaking novel missions, and have access to different resources and capabilities than in their academic lives.

Other examples challenge the idea that one must have any credentials at all for true scholarship. Parents or patients have independently pursued data and generated hypotheses for rare diseases with no prior knowledge about biology or medicine. They undoubtedly became much more scholarly than the majority of PhDs in the world about that specific topic.[2]

Some independent scholars have taken to creative avenues to fund dissemination of their work without the typical institutional grant money that academics use.[3] There are organizations that offer funding, research facilities and guidance available to pursue projects with commercial or social promise, and communities for independent scholars and scientists not affiliated with an academic institution.[4]

Some people lament the very term "independent scholar" the same way many raise a brow at the term "woman professor." The "independent" adjective implies abnormality—a rogue identity hurtling past the orbits of social normalcy.

But this is precisely where change begins. As the number of independent scholars inevitably continues to grow over the next decade, we will accumulate a critical mass of interested individuals willing to drive change that will benefit all.

Bringing different backgrounds, motivations, viewpoints, and networks to scholarship is a good thing, because no one has a monopoly on discovery and truth. As independent scholars meeting the world outside the ivory tower, we can help to make that world a better place by having been a part of academia. We can find ever more ways to support or contribute to academia, even as we are no longer limited by its rules and traditions.

A Lesson of Seventy Kicks: Just Do It

One of the very real benefits of finding full-time employment is having a steady paycheck that provides the stability and financial means to pursue hobbies, among other things. I spent some of that paycheck to get myself back into fitness and martial arts, something I had tried out and enjoyed in graduate school.

I ended up picking up striking, also known as stand-up martial arts. It's composed of what you'd think: learning how to kick, punch, block, and use your elbows and knees. After learning the basics with a great instructor over the course of six months, I joined a small sparring group with a few other students, applying exercises and techniques we practiced solo in free-flowing mini-matches.

During one of those lessons, our teacher asked us to do a warm-up exercise: perform seventy roundhouse kicks in under two minutes.

He invited a fellow student, a quiet, petite woman, to try the exercise.

She shook her head. "I can't," she protested.

Just doing seventy kicks in a row sounded preposterous. Executing seventy kicks in under two minutes meant that each kick had to be completed in less than two seconds. It didn't sound possible.

He gave an exasperated laugh. "Just do it," he urged, waggling the thick Thai pad targets strapped to his arms. He braced them into position to receive her kicks.

"I know you can do it. Just go."

After a moment of doubtful consideration, she got into her

fighting stance and started with one kick, and then the next. We all started counting as she kept going . . .

. . . two . . . three . . . four . . .

. . . getting louder and louder . . .

. . . fifteen . . . sixteen . . .

. . . twenty-three! . . . twenty-four! . . . and before we knew it we were shouting and she had completed thirty-five on one leg and the instructor yelled "Switch!" and she switched to her other leg and kept going.

She completed seventy roundhouse kicks in under two minutes.

And when she was done she was gasping, but smiling. We all were.

"See?" he said, pleased. "That wasn't so bad. You could do it all along."

Over the last five years, I've spent a lot of free time coaching fellow doctorates on their job hunts through Free the PhD. I've seen a lot of people who are perfectly capable of admirable, frankly kick-ass, things stop themselves from executing their own seventy kicks.

We have so many excuses not to take action on our own behalf.

"No one responds to my applications."

"Recruiters are too business oriented and don't know what to do with me."

"I have no idea where to start."

"People tell me I'm overqualified for entry-level jobs, but that I don't have enough experience for the jobs that want PhDs."

"Networking is awkward; I don't like bothering people."

"I'm too busy to do job applications right now."

"I don't know what's out there."

These are very real, very common mental blocks we face as PhDs tackling the job market. The key, though, is to gather structural knowledge early, and allow yourself the courage and self-confidence to get better, one step (or kick or application or cold email) at a time.

No one knows how to execute seventy roundhouse kicks without actually standing in front of a heavy bag and physically lifting their leg, shifting their weight, and making contact with the bag for the very first time.

No PhD knows how to talk to recruiters, impress hiring managers, expand their network with total strangers, or give stunning job talks, without first taking action to determine what drives their passions, studying the job market, and figuring out what people are hiring for and why.

If you have not thought deeply about what makes you happy, as opposed to what you are "supposed to be" doing, you cannot define and set personal priorities. This is the first conversation I have with most PhDs trying to find their path outside academia. If you are chasing someone else's definition of success when your preferences don't align, you are setting yourself up for failure.

I also find that academics do not usually network early in their training or careers, but wait until they are desperate for a job. By doing this, you cut yourself off from genuine relationships and will never hear about the hidden opportunities communicated internally by employees of organizations. You deny yourself the chance to meet potential advocates and friends, and resign yourself to the most difficult, distasteful, and failure-prone kind of networking—asking strangers for a job. Don't do this!

Most importantly, you may be afraid to try on a new identity, for no good reason other than the fact that it's unknown to you.

But we are academics, scholars, researchers, and scientists. We face and conquer the unknown every single day, through exploration, experimentation, and analysis.

We conquer our career challenges the same way.

PhDs have been transitioning into successful, happy lives after their research trainee experiences—either into faculty positions or other jobs—for decades. Some go to research-heavy positions adjacent to their academic lives. Some leave their research behind as they forge a new identity with the help of their previous experiences.

Success lies not in where you go, but more in how you get there and what you do once you've arrived at your next destination. Ideally, you can do what I have done, and entwine your love for scholarship and research with the power of your passions. Look forward to new directions that truly make you excited to get out of bed every morning.

Some PhDs fear what their colleagues or classmates might think of them after they leave academia. Yet that fear is usually unfounded, because so many other factors will be in play. You'll be in a new field, with new goals and new colleagues who share a different view of success than your academic colleagues.

Even as someone who has transitioned to the "dark side," I have no qualms interacting with researchers, and have never felt uncomfortable going back to labs to talk with academic PhDs. When I interact with academics, I can still speak their language. But what's different is that now I can also speak the language of business, entrepreneurship, and advocacy, reaching many more people whose views I share. I have not lost the academic perspective, but have gained new understandings of how the world works.

Purposefully directing your career focus and actively evolving a unique professional identity is not only normal, but in fact the scientifically data-driven thing to do in our modern world. This kind of self-awareness is doubly important for anyone who has been secluded in one specialized line of work for a long time—be it a professional athlete, veteran, or fellow researcher.

PhDs are now more vulnerable than ever in the fast-shifting landscape of the modern workplace. We must compete with those who have been learning to ride the waves of change from the beginning of their careers, often with fewer years left in our working life to catch up. We face more doubt and resistance when we are applying for jobs for the same reason we are valuable— because we bring a different experience set to the table. But the funny thing about the concepts of "winning and losing," "success and failure," is that they are entirely and completely relative. The reality is that we are each the entrepreneur of our own careers, the founder of our futures. Let's be brave enough to forge our own identities, and get out there to disrupt the world. #FreeThePhD

NOTES

1. Cambridge Dictionary (Cambridge University Press), s.v. "scholar," accessed May 2019, https://dictionary.cambridge.org/dictionary/english /scholar.

2. Conor Gearin, "Children with Rare Genetic Disease Inspire Parents to Find Cure," PBS, April 12, 2016, https://www.pbs.org/wgbh/nova /article/children-with-rare-genetic-disease-inspire-parents-to-find -cure/; "A Young Reporter Chronicles Her 'Brain on Fire,'" NPR, November 14, 2012, https://www.npr.org/2012/11/14/165115921/a-young -reporter-chronicles-her-brain-on-fire; Seth Mnookin, "Fighting a One- of-a-Kind Disease," *New Yorker*, July 14, 2014, https://www.newyorker .com/magazine/2014/07/21/one-of-a-kind-2.

3. Backyard Brains, "Backyard Brains: Operation Publication," Kick- starter, December 29, 2011, https://www.kickstarter.com/projects/back yardbrains/backyard-brains-operation-publication.

4. "Grants," Chan Zuckerberg Initiative, accessed May 20, 2019, https://chanzuckerberg.com/grants-ventures/grants/; IndieBio, accessed May 20, 2019, https://indiebio.co; National Coalition of Independent Scholars, accessed May 20, 2019, https://www.ncis.org/national-coalition -independent-scholars-ncis; Citizen Science Association, accessed May 20, 2019, https://www.citizenscience.org/.

Contributors

Christine Caccipuoti received her BA and MA in history from Fordham University and has served as assistant producer of the podcast *Footnoting History* since its inception in 2013. She displays her love of biography by covering the extraordinary lives of Napoleon Bonaparte's family and England's early Plantagenet royals for *Footnoting History* and through publications like her entry about Blanche Caldwell Barrow for *American National Biography*. In addition, Christine is a member of SAG-AFTRA and the Actors' Equity Association. More about her can be found on ChristineCaccipuoti.com.

Vay Cao, PhD, is the Asia Pacific sales manager at a neurotechnology company and founder of Free the PhD. She loves traveling, educating, and enabling the commercialization of cutting-edge technology for the betterment of scientific innovation and human health. Vay spends her free time running Free the PhD, which helps researchers find a life they love outside academia, just as she has. You can check out Free the PhD at FreethePhD.com, or join her and fellow Freed PhDs for personalized career guidance and a supportive community at FreethePhD.mn.co.

Joshua Hevert, PhD, currently holds the position of instructor of history at Cotton Valley Early College High School in Fabens, Texas, a small rural town just outside of El Paso. He also teaches several classes as an adjunct for El Paso Community College. Dr. Hevert received his PhD in medieval history from the University of North Carolina at Chapel Hill in 2016. At Cotton Valley Early College, Dr. Hevert teaches both the US history and pre-AP world history surveys. He is the sponsor of the class of 2020 and of their chapter of the National Honor Society. He is married to Dr. Melissa Esmacher, an associate professor of history at El Paso Community College. They have four dogs: Joy, Sippi, Drexler, and Mateo.

Katherine Anderson Howell is a 2018 Pushcart Prize nominee, the editor of *Fandom as Classroom Practice: A Teaching Guide* (2018), and an esthiology student at the Aveda Institute of the South in Washington, DC. Her scholarly work can be found in places like the *Journal of Fandom Studies*, where she recently guest-edited an issue on disability, and *Pennsylvania English*. Her creative work can be found in *Rumpus, Stillwater Review, Beltway Poetry Quarterly, Account, Misfit Magazine,* and *Mojave Heart Review*, among others. Follow her on Twitter @GenKatieOrgana.

Alison Innes received two BAs, one in history from York University and one in Classics from McMaster University, and an MA in Classics from Brock University. In addition to her primary occupation as a social media manager at Brock University in Ontario, Canada, she also does freelance work in both higher education and social media. In her free time she is a practicing artist and the producer and cohost of the podcast *MythTake*. She can be found on social media @InnesAlison.

Elizabeth Keohane-Burbridge earned her MA and PhD in medieval history from Fordham University. Since 2013, she has been the producer of, and contributor to, *Footnoting History* (FootnotingHistory.com), a popular history podcast that boasts over two million downloads and twenty thousand subscribers. Her work has been published in *Medieval Prosopography* and *Nursing Clio*. She has presented at multiple international conferences about her personal research interests and about podcasting. Elizabeth serves on the Lifelong Community Advisory Board and chairs the Neighbors Committee for the city of Decatur, Georgia. She teaches history at Woodward Academy, an independent school in College Park, Georgia. For more information, please see woodward.academia.edu /ElizabethKeohaneBurbridge or follow her on Twitter @HistorianMum.

Dayanna Knight, PhD, is an art instructor, author, and illustrator specializing in the early medieval world. Dr. Knight is the creator of the Viking Coloring Book Project, which seeks to allow children of all ages to explore the past while coloring themselves into history. The primary focus of the VCB Project is to utilize public outreach to safely grow interest in the early medieval period beyond negative stereotyping. The first title, *The Viking Coloring Book*, was published in 2017.

Laura A. Macaluso researches and writes about material culture, monuments, murals, and museums. Her recent work includes coordinating and editing the publication of *Monument Culture: International Perspectives on the Future of Monuments in a Changing World* (2019) and preparing for the upcoming volume on the public art of Hartford, Connecticut, for Wesleyan University Press. Curatorial projects focus on exhibits reflective of community interests, including the first community mural program in New Haven, Connecticut, and the emotional upheaval around the display of a Confederate battle flag in Lynchburg, Virginia. She works as a grant writer for history, art, and park organizations in Virginia and Connecticut. Laura tweets as @HistoricLore; more about Laura can be found at LauraMacaluso.com.

Allyson Schettino has a BA and MA from Fordham University and has worked in museum education for eleven years. She is the associate director of school programs at the New-York Historical Society Museum & Library, where she oversees museum and outreach programs for students from pre-K through college. She also writes curriculum guides for teaching American history in K–12 classrooms. You can find her favorite project, Women & the American Story, at wams.nyhistory.org. She thanks her parents for their enduring support, her husband for his love and patience, and her daughter for making the world a brighter place.

Valerie Schutte earned her PhD in history from the University of Akron. She is author of *Mary I and the Art of Book Dedications: Royal Women,*

Power, and Persuasion (2015) and editor or coeditor of four volumes of essays on queenship, heirs, and Shakespeare. She has published articles and book chapters on royal Tudor women and the history of the book. She is currently completing a monograph comparing Princesses Mary and Elizabeth Tudor, is coediting a volume on Mary I as represented in writing and literature, and is undertaking a large-scale investigation of the life and afterlife of Anne of Cleves.

Danielle T. Slaughter is an academic turned mommy. She has her BA from the University of Michigan–Ann Arbor and an MA in English from Georgia State University. With a doctoral background in English, focusing on rhetoric and composition, Danielle likes to call herself and mothers like her "Mamademics." Mamademics is a merging of her two "careers"—motherhood and academia. She lives in Atlanta with her husband and two sons, where she runs her award-winning parenting blog, *Mamademics*, and its social justice consultant spin-off, Mamademics Academy.

Index